Life in the Pressure Cooker

Life in the Pressure Cooker

Roy R. Roberts

Studies in James

BMH Books

Winona Lake, Indiana 46590

DEDICATION

To Rev. Michael R. Ryan and Donna Sue, his "rib," who are dear friends of God and precious friends of ours. Mike is my co-laborer in the service of our Lord Jesus Christ. Pastor Mike Ryan is a former USC All-American and professional football player.

Cover design and art: Tim Kennedy

ISBN: 0-88469-036-9

COPYRIGHT 1977
BMH BOOKS
WINONA LAKE, INDIANA

Printed in U.S.A.

Acknowledgments

I thank the Lord for Patty, my partner, who shares everything with me, including the work on this manuscript. I wish to credit my daughter, Dawn Marie, for her patience, as her mother and I labored on the manuscript. The needs of an eight year old are not met by a typewriter.

I am grateful to the editors of the New American Standard Bible. All quotations from the Word of God, which appear in this book, are taken from this classic translation, unless otherwise designated.

The manifold contributions of Dr. James E. Rosscup, professor of Bible Exposition at Talbot Theological Seminary, are forever with me. He is quoted throughout this work for it is impossible for me to improve on the finest of Biblical scholarship exhibited by this man of God.

The faculties of John Brown University, Siloam Springs, Arkansas; and Biola College and its graduate school, Talbot Theological Seminary in La Mirada, California, were immense to me.

I would also like to acknowledge the beautiful people of the Grace Brethren Church of Seal Beach, California, who are a joy to lead in the Lord Jesus Christ. It is because of their doing the work of service that the congregation is experiencing a growth explosion (Eph. 4:11-16).

I am eternally indebted to the Holy Spirit, who did for me exactly what the Lord Jesus said the Spirit would do: "But when He, the Spirit of truth, comes, He will guide you into all the truth; for He will not speak on His own initiative, but whatever He hears, He will speak; and He will disclose to you what is to come. He shall glorify Me; for He shall take of Mine, and shall disclose it to you" (John 16:13-14).

Then last, but foremost, I acknowledge the Lord Jesus Christ Himself, who is the reason for my existence and for this book (Col. 1:18, Gal. 2:20, Phil. 1:21). May He receive the greater glory (yea, all the glory) for these pages (Rev. 4:11).

Introductory Remarks

Unless otherwise designated, all Scripture passages and references are from the New American Standard Bible.

Words contained in parentheses are from the Koine Greek, the common language of the original New Testament.

The book contains thirteen chapters in order that productive study might be facilitated by means of one chapter per week. Therefore, the author has divided the Book of James into thirteen segments. Each segment is given an individual outline for the purpose of presenting greater concentration for that particular part of God's Word. For the purpose of uniformity and continuity, the Book of James may be understood in the following brief, expository outline:

I.   The PRELUDE to the Book of James, 1:1.

II. The PRESENCE of testings and temptations, 1:1-20.
    A.   The aim of testing, 1:2-12
    B.   The attitude toward temptations, 1:13-20.

III. The PATTERN of faith in action, 1:21—4:17.
    A.   Faith receives the word, 1:21-27.
    B.   Faith produces impartiality, 2:1-13.
    C.   Faith produces works of sharing, 2:14-26.
    D.   Faith controls the tongue, 3:1-12.
    E.   Faith produces works of divine wisdom, 3:13-18.
    F.   Faith replaces worldliness with subjection to God, 4:1-17.

IV. The PROSPECT of faith, 5:1-20.
    A.   The certainty of judgment upon the unsaved rich, 5:1-6.
    B.   The consolation to persecuted believers, 5:7-20.

Table of Contents

Pressure, Pressure, Pressure

THE CHAPTER OUTLINED:

Trials and testing are like a rugged football practice, they produce endurance in the "long fourth quarter" (James 1:12).

When a man is "out-of-shape" or not prepared for an athletic contest, the last quarter can be so long that it seems like forever. Certain branches of the armed forces, and some football coaches, adhere to the philosophy that the most mileage can be obtained from a man if you tear him down and then build him up again. Needless to say, that in the secular world, this tearing down may result even in dehumanization. God will never allow this (I Cor. 10:13; II Peter 2:9) when trials come upon the Christian.

The believer needs the "Divine Perspective" when it comes to trials and testings. Indeed, it is most difficult to accept that God permits continuing difficulty for the Christian (James 1:1-4, 12-15).

It is true that the Christian life *is not* a bed of roses. There are wonderful experiences symbolized by the petals as well as the daily hassles portrayed by the thorns. Life is a "long fourth quarter" and God places us in difficult practice sessions so that our endurance will be great and we will come out strong for the contest.

I. THE PRELUDE TO THE BOOK, 1:1

"James" is immediately identified as the writer. Paul refers to him as "James the Lord's brother" (Gal. 1:19). James was the son of Mary and Joseph. The Lord Jesus was virgin born (Matt. 1:20-23); hence, He was the *literal* son of Mary, and the *legal* son of Joseph. Mary was a virgin until she gave birth to the Lord Jesus Christ (Matt. 1:25). But, after the birth of Christ, Mary and Joseph had other children, some of whom were James (the human author of the New Testament book which bears his name), Joseph, Judas (not Iscariot; but the writer of the Book of Jude), and Simon (Matt. 13:55-56).

John, the apostle, says, "For not even His brothers were believing in Him" (John 7:5). Evidently James did not realize who Jesus was. Imagine living with a perfect half brother, who later claimed to be the promised Messiah. That would be a little bit hard to take. But, when Christ returned from the dead, James became a strong believer since he was evidently converted by the risen Lord (I Cor. 15:7). As a matter of fact, James became the pastor-teacher of the church in Jerusalem. He was a heavy duty person and strongly aggressive in his faith (Acts 12:17; 15:13-29; 21:17-18).

The name "James" (*Iakobos*) is the English form of the Greek word for Jacob, meaning "heel-gripper." One might say that one Jacob is writing to another Jacob, which are "the twelve tribes who are dispersed abroad." (See Gen. 29-30 and 40 for a list of the sons of Jacob). James recognized that even in the first century of the church some Israelis, from each of the twelve tribes, had met their Messiah. These Jewish Christians were being greatly persecuted under Saul of Tarsus. These believers had to flee in terror from their beloved Jerusalem. They became "dispersed abroad." They were the *diaspora* of James 1:1. James wants to prepare them for the pressures of life, so he gives the purpose of testing in verses 2-4.

James was not a stranger to persecution for he was "a bond-servant of God and of the Lord Jesus Christ" and therefore was a target for persecution. "Bond-servant" literally is "to bind." He was a Christian to the core for he was bound to Christ. He was Christ's man—lock, stock and barrel. He was the Saviour's slave and he was to pay dearly for it; even with his life.

II. THE PURPOSE OF TESTING, 1:2-4

The word "that" in verse 4 alerts the readers to the purpose of trials "that you may be perfect and complete, lacking in nothing." Therefore, not just the persecuted *diaspora*, but all brethren must "consider it all joy when you encounter various trials" (1:2).

"All joy" appears first in the word order of the original Greek and is therefore the point of emphasis. Someone has defined "joy" as that Christian good cheer which results from the confidence that your resources in Christ are adequate. No matter what the circumstances of life, the Christian's good cheer is grounded in the resources of Christ. All hell may break loose, but the Christian should be joyous because Christ is sufficient. His purposes for the believer are good (Rom. 8:28).

The word "consider" means to take the lead (Acts 14:12), or to command (Matt. 2:6; Acts 7:10). The noun form described a leader who does the thinking like a quarterback who "calls the plays." The word may mean simply "to think, count or esteem" (Acts 26:2; II Cor. 9:5). Therefore James is saying that even in the most nightmarish persecution, the believer can be in command of his thoughts.

One day I was helping a friend move from one home to another; we rented a truck. After we had loaded the truck, we wondered what to do with the fish aquarium. Very unintelligently, we placed the aquarium on the front seat of the truck including the fish and water. When we were bumping down the freeway at 55 mph, water began splashing and gushing everywhere until the both of us were soaked. But those little fish were as buoyant and peaceful in their aquarium as they possibly could be. This illustrates what James means by "consider it all joy when you encounter various trials." There needs to be a believer's bouyancy and a sense of well-being when he lives from resources that are adequate in the Lord Jesus Christ.

Verse 3 states, "Knowing that the testing of your faith produces endurance." There are two Greek words which are translated by the one English word "know" in the New Testament, one revealing more of a "head knowledge"; whereas the other portrays a knowledge by experience. James uses the latter in verse 3. And...as one knows by experience some of the horrors of hassle (and the present tense shows that this is the pattern of life), it produces endurance. Trials are faith-testers. If the faith is genuine saving faith, then that faith will produce endurance, in the crucible of life. "Endurance" is that quality of life that perseveres and never gives up no matter what the circumstances. Christ is the perfect example, for Paul attests: "And may the Lord direct your hearts into the love of God and into the steadfastness of Christ" (II Thess. 3:5). What James is saying is what Paul wrote about in Romans 5:3-4, "...but we also exult in our tribulations; knowing that tribulation brings about perseverance; and perseverance, proven character...."

Verse 4 reinforces this idea concerning the end result of trials. Tribulation is a character-developer; in the words of James it is the "perfect result." This character that trials produce, this "perfect result," is spelled out by James in three ways: (1) "Perfect"—the word doesn't mean sinless, but is a word that depicts a process. That process is becoming more like Christ and progressively moving away from evil. It is Christian maturity (Rom. 8:29). John describes perfection this way, "and every one who has this hope fixed on Him purifies himself..." (I John 3:3). (2) "Complete"—this is a compound word in the original from *holos* meaning whole or complete and *kleros* which is assigned or allotted. It therefore means sound in all of its parts like the lame man who was healed in Acts 3:16. Character and maturity are characteristics of a solid Christian. (3) "Lacking in nothing"—this is simply the negative aspect of what the Lord's brother has already stated positively. It does add weight to his point; however, if a believer is lacking then he needs to begin at the place of prayer.

III. THE PRAYER DURING TESTING, 1:5

Many times I have asked God "Why do I have to go through this trial?" "Why did You allow that?" Why, Why, Why!!! I, like many others, have needed the "Divine Viewpoint" on trials.

Trials can be very discouraging. They can defeat brothers and sisters in Christ. They also can produce resentment and anger toward God. "Throwing in the towel" may seem tremendously easier than persevering in trials. How many times I have heard someone say as I counseled in my office, "I cannot cope with that problem, that trial." One man said, "How can a God of love do that to me?" God's perspective answers all of these questions and more. Christians need wisdom from God. God, in turn, delights to give to them all that they need. J. B. Phillips has caught the essence of James' words in his apt paraphrase, "If...any of you does not know how to meet any particular problem...."

Friend, just ask the Lord. He gives "generously." The word from which this adverb is derived means "to spread out, to reach." God's hand is stretched forth and he wants to give to us without reserve. Jesus taught that God gives with "good measure, pressed down, shaken together, running over, they will pour into your lap..." (Luke 6:38). He also gives "without reproach." God doesn't heap insults upon the man who comes to Him in need. James E. Rosscup comments:

> One might give a gift and make the recipient feel like dirt under his feet. He crams his unworthiness down his throat and reminds him of his own goodness. God does not give like this! One might give and then pester the recipient with endless reminders lest he forget, or nag him for failing to show his gratitude.

God is both forthright in the *manner* and unstinting in the *measure* of His giving.

What is God giving? It is wisdom (*sophia*). Recall that the bishop of Jerusalem is writing to the Jews of the *diaspora*—those scattered because they followed Christ. Their pressures were great. Wisdom was promised through the power of God's indwelling Holy Spirit. In the words of Spiros Zodiates:

> He does not speak of the wisdom as the world thinks of it, but speaks of the necessity of the Holy Spirit's indwelling every believer and then, and only then, can the Christian be the master of circumstances. Unless there is within us that which is above us, we shall soon yield to that which is about us.

This wisdom is simply and tersely seeing things as God sees them; it is having the "Divine Perspective" on trials. Brethren, never cease to be thankful to God for His encouragement in the midst of trial. God's viewpoint is desperately needed in times of trials. Here on the West Coast, the testimony of Merrill Womach, a resident of Spokane, Washington, is well known. On Thanksgiving Day, 1961, Merrill was flying in his private plane. A tragic crash followed by fire resulted in the complete destruction of Mr. Womach's face. The pain was so severe that he literally tore his seat belt from its anchor, since the fire had ruined the buckle and it would not open. As he staggered from the forest, a service station attendant was quoted as saying that Merrill's head had swollen three times its normal size and looked like a roasted marshmallow. Having undergone fifty operations to date, Merrill gives glory to God. The incredible report from those who transported him to the hospital relates Merrill as singing hymns to the Lord even though his head was decimated in flame. The film "He Restoreth My Soul" has been a blessing to many as it unfolds Womach's unreal tale of perseverance in trials. Mr. Womach had the "Divine Perspective" and still does. This is readily seen in:

IV. THE PRIORITY OF FAITH IN TESTING, 1:6-8

James is writing to God's people in the midst of death and distress, trial and conflict, who live in a strife-torn world. George Sweeting says, "he deals with the nitty gritty of life, and he tells us that a faith with *works* is a faith that *lasts*." Faith is priority number one in testings and especially in a man's asking for God-given wisdom.

Martin Luther, however, felt that James was a "straw epistle." He believed that the book majored in *works* and therefore it contradicted the Epistle to the Romans which emphasized faith. On the other hand, John Wesley said that James spoke of faith from beginning (1:5) to end (5:15). In reality, James' discussion of works does not contradict Paul's teachings on this doctrine, but complements it from the practical point of view.

Perhaps some of those who had been dispersed throughout the Roman Empire by persecution had prayed and nothing happened. They were praying sometimes believing and sometimes not (1:6). Their manner of praying was incorrect. A man cannot be "double-minded" and expect God to give him the "Divine Viewpoint"; in other words, wisdom.

The correct method of prayer is to "ask in faith without any doubting." This does not mean that God is a "Give-Me-Machine" or a "Glorified Bellhop" who comes at one's every beck and call. One cannot pray like Augustine, "Lord make me pure, but not yet." He is "the Lord" (1:7), and, as such, He will honor those who are sensitive to His terms; namely, faith.

Faith is "without any doubting"—and James Ropes says that means to be "at variance with one's self." Joseph Mayor describes this doubting man as a cork floating on the wave, now carried toward the shore, now away from it.

Verse 8 says that the doubter is "double-minded" or "two-souled." Alexander Ross says, "He is virtually a man with two souls, which are in conflict with each other.... Such a man is unstable and unreliable in all his ways, and not merely in the realm of prayer." This man tries to live for God and hold onto the world at the same time. This is why Christians crackup and develop hang-ups of all kinds. The Lord said that one cannot serve God and Mammon (Matt. 6:24; Luke 16:13). This is the essence of the two-souled man. He is a man of divided allegiances. He has mental reservations both about prayer itself and about the requests he makes of God. Such a man "cannot hope to receive anything from God" (Phillips). It may be of interest to the reader to note another reason why some prayer requests are not granted by the Lord as recorded in James 4:3.

V. THE PARTICIPANTS IN TESTINGS, 1:9-11

The wealthy and the poor stand equally before the Lord, who has one requirement—faith. They both participate in testings. Faith itself requires a careful evaluation of what really counts in life. If a man's true wealth is in the Lord, then his concern will not be riches in this life (I Tim. 6:9)—whether he is a poor man or a rich man. God's perspective is that "things" are transitory—they pass away. Therefore, contentment is to be seen in a life of faith (II Cor. 6; 12:9-10; Phil. 4:6-13; I Tim. 6:6-7; I John 2:17).

The secret of the Christian life is simply that a man is high when he is low (1:9) because his height is in Christ. But, the man who trusts in riches will be brought down (Matt. 19:23). The rich pass away like the flower which comes and goes (1:10). The destiny of the unsaved rich man is painted in verse 11 (cf. Isa. 40:7-8; I Peter 1:24). In my travels to the lands of the Bible, I have discovered that grass stays green for only a brief period of time. The Middle Eastern "sun rises with a scorching wind, and withers the grass; and its flower falls off, and the beauty of its appearance is destroyed..." (1:11). The rich will come and go just like the green grass of Palestine when the sirocco blows and generates the heat. For James says, "...so too the rich man in the midst of his pursuits will fade away" (1:11). "Pursuits" means "walkings or journeyings." It depicts the constant endeavors of a man to obtain riches—it is an obsession. He "will fade away." Another way of translating this would be that "he will be worn out."

The man with God's viewpoint knows that his life is secured by sure things rooted in the Lord, things which he can never lose. Things do go better with Christ. Someone asked concerning a wealthy man, who passed away, "How much did he leave?" The answer was, "He left it all. There are no pockets in shrouds."

But how does all of this tie into the discussion of testings?

VI. THE PRIZE AT THE END OF TESTINGS, 1:12

The life of faith pays off in blessedness. James says, "Blessed is a man who perseveres under trial...." The word "blessed" is a popularly used New Testament word and means "happy." It may also mean "born again" (Matt. 5:3-11). The individual, therefore, in James 1:12 who is blessed is one who shares the very nature of God. That is part of the reason why he is so happy.

He is a brother who perseveres under trial. When the pressures of life are great, this one "hangs tough." As Paul confirms, "But in all these things we overwhelmingly conquer through Him who loved us" (Rom. 8:37). In other words, happy is the man who "hangs in there" when bombarded by difficulties. The present tense is employed in the verb "persevere" in verse 12. It indicates that pressures and problems exist right now and is the norm for the life of the brethren.

The reward for perseverance is the approval of the Lord Jesus Himself. The conquering Christian will be rewarded with the Crown of Life, which the Lord Jesus has promised to those who love Him. Actually it is those who are loving as a habit of life since the present tense is again used. Ross says that the word approved "was often used by Greek writers to describe coins which have been tested and shown to be genuine." Related to persons, this idea of being approved is the way other people see Christianity's character and practicality in one's relationship to God.

The approved one will receive the crown of life. This is the crown of the winner, the victor, the one who persevers. R. V. G. Tasker elucidates:

> The love of the Christian for his Lord does not win for him eternal life as a reward to which he has a right, any more than does his faith. It is, however, an axiom of the Bible that God has abundant blessings in store for those who *love Him*, keep His commandments, and serve Him faithfully whatever the cost may be (see Matt. 19:28; I Cor. 2:9).

In other words, God offers salvation to the lost; and to the Christian who serves faithfully, God offers rewards. Salvation is a free gift (John 4:10; Rom. 6:23; Eph. 2:8-9; Titus 3:5-7); whereas rewards are earned by works (Matt. 10:42; Luke 19:17; I Cor. 9:24-25; II Tim. 4:7-8; Rev. 2:10;

22:12).

There are a variety of crowns with which the Lord will reward His believers when He calls them to be with Himself. Christ rewards faithfulness of all types by means of crowns. It is most intriguing that, according to the New Testament (Rev. 4:9-11), when the believer sees Christ, and stands in His presence, he will cast his crowns before the Lord. He alone is worthy to receive all praise and glory.

If your faith, dear reader, is genuine and approved by God, you *will* persevere. You *will* be continually loving the Lord. You *will* be a winner. A familiar story is told of a man who was trying to express his love to a woman over the telephone. He said, "I will die without you. I will climb the highest mountain and swim the widest ocean for you. I will do anything for you." Then he said, "I'll come over to see you tonight if it doesn't rain." Christ will reward those who persevere in the rain or sun. Perseverence is the normal Christian experience.

The Tragedy of Lust

2

THE CHAPTER OUTLINED:

I. The **RATIONALIZATION** in Temptations, 1:13-16
    A. The **CAUSE** of Temptation, 1:13-14
    B. The **CULMINATION** of Sin, 1:15
    C. The **CONSEQUENCES** of Sin, 1:15
    D. The **CONCERN** We Need, 1:16

II. The **RECOGNITION** of God and His Gifts, 1:17-18
    A. The **CHARACTERISTICS** of God's Gifts, 1:17
    B. The **CHARACTER** of God Himself, 1:17
    C. His **COMPASSION** in Salvation, 1:18
        1. The **POWER** of Regeneration, 1:18
        2. The **PURPOSE** of Regeneration, 1:18

III. The **RESULT** of Regeneration, 1:19

IV. The **RECEPTION** of the Word of God, 1:20

Football players have an expression for an illegal or late hit. They call it a "cheap shot." Generally a "dirty player" is characterized as a "cheap shot artist." Many times he is successful in his activities because the officials do not detect him in the act. Lust to the Christian is a lot like the cheap shot which gets him when he is not looking or when his defenses are down or where he is most vulnerable.

We all need to understand the nature and character of lust. There are dangers in rationalization in which one tends to blame everything and everybody for his own responsibility in yielding to lust as a form of temptation.

I. THE RATIONALIZATION IN TEMPTATIONS, 1:13-16

A. The CAUSE of Temptation, 1:13-14. In James, chapter 1, the concepts of trials and temptations come from the same word in the Greek. In verses 1 through 12, the noun form is used which conveys the idea of external adversities brought about by means of the outward circumstances of life. Verses 13 and following use the verb, which indicates the inner impulse to evil, the subjective solicitation to sin; hence, "temptation." Temptation is common to man (I Cor. 10:13) in that it comes from within.

Now who is responsible for temptation? When James writes about this, he probably had in mind the Jewish concept of the *yetzer ha ra'* (that is, "evil impulse"). We must remember that he is writing to Jews who have been converted to Christ. "Some Jews reasoned that since God created everything, He must have created the evil impulse. And since it is the evil impulse that tempts man to sin, ultimately God, who created it, is responsible for evil" (Walter W. Wessel).

This is just like a lot of Christians today. Rosscup writes:

> Some resort to lying to get themselves out of a jam; they burst out with foul language in exasperation; they steal or cheat others to make up for hard times; they harbor festering resentments against others; they indulge in self-pity and bitter complaining; they cannot for a period have normal sexual relations with their married partners and so satisfy their urges in immoral affairs with others. Then they blithely shift the blame for their sin to God and acquit themselves of any fault.

It is said of President Harry S. Truman that there was a sign on his desk which read: "The Buck Stops Here." That meant that he took full responsibility for the activities of his administration. When it comes to sin in our lives, the buck stops right at our doorstep.

Adam tried to blame God and Eve both for his first sin. "The *woman* whom *Thou* gavest to be with me, *she* gave me from the tree, and I ate" (Gen. 3:12). This was Adam's cop-out. He would not take the responsibility for his own actions but tried to rationalize his way out of it. Believe it or not Eve did the same thing. She said, "The *serpent* deceived me, and I ate" (Gen. 3:13). Everybody was blaming everybody else. The poet illustrates this:

> Thou knowest Thou hast formed me with passions wild and strong; And listening to their witching voice has often led me wrong.
> (Robert Burns)

It is always easier to blame God or someone else when we get into trouble. The Israelis did this to Moses. Nowhere in the Great Book of God do we see the Lord trying to make plans to mess us up. He is not scheming to bring us defeat. If He does not do it, then who does?

God is not the cause of a man's fall into sin. God does not place into the heart of anyone the direct desire to sin. The responsibility for sin lies squarely on the shoulder of the one who committed it. It is not *society's* fault, a *spouse's* fault, *Satan's* fault or the *Saviour's* fault—the cause of *sin* is *self*.

As verse 13 of chapter 1 clearly teaches, due to the character of God it is impossible He should become implicated in evil. And because of this, it is absolutely absurd to regard God as causing any man to do evil. Lust comes from within. Promiscuity is nothing more than a man or woman being guided by his glands. This one lives by the injunction: "If you feel the urge, splurge!" God doesn't guide us by our glands; but by the Holy Spirit. Simply stated, "He Himself does not tempt any one" (v. 13).

The answer is both Satan and ourselves. The first two chapters of Job show us this more clearly. The great thing about Job is that he did not err in charging God foolishly. Where does sin originate? Do not look to anyone else. To do so would be immature judgment. There is a need for accepting personal responsibility for our actions.

Verse 14 tersely calls a spade a spade. A man's own lust carries him away and entices him. The words "carried away" are from the root (*exeikos*) "to drag away from." The word means to drag or draw, as some were dragged out of the temple (Acts 21:30), as rich men draw some into court (James 2:6), as no one can come to Christ unless the Fathers draws (or attracts) him (John 6:44). Indeed, the world is attractive with all its glitter, tinsel and lights and it can draw one away seductively and sweetly. The old sin nature is easily allured.

The word "enticed" is also most graphic. It means "to lure" and is from a root with the idea of "bait." It appears also in II Peter 2:14 and 18. Lust is like bait which disguises a deadly hook so that a fish is deceived to bite.

Soon after Augustine's conversion, he was walking down the street in Milan, Italy. There he accosted a prostitute whom he had known most intimately. She called but he would not answer. He kept right on walking. "Augustine," she called again. "It is I!" Without slowing down, but with assurance of Christ in his heart, he testified, "Yes, but it is no longer I." Although young in the faith, he knew something of a solicitation to do evil and the way of victory over temptation. His reply, "It is no longer I," expresses a realization that he had a new power available to combat the forces of sin and evil which would seek to dominate his life. He was a changed man. This is the essence of verses 13-20. In the words of the Master, "Keep watching and praying, that you may not enter into temptation; the spirit is willing, but the flesh is weak" (Matt. 26:41).

Just exactly what is lust? Basically it denotes wrong desire (II Peter 1:4; II Tim. 3:6; Titus 3:3) or an illicit craving and is the same word translated "covet" elsewhere in the Scriptures (Rom. 13:9). It is associated with all of the multifaceted desires and cravings of the soul. Sin results because our old sin nature craves wickedness (Eph. 2:3). This comes to us in three areas of temptation: "For all that is in the world, the lust of the flesh and the lust of the eyes and the boastful pride of life, is not from the Father, but is from the world (I John 2:16). The desire to enjoy things can become the lust of the flesh; the desire to get things can become the lust of the eyes; and the desire to do things can become the boastful pride of life. The temptation of Eve was within this threefold area. The fruit was good to eat, good to possess, and good to make one wise. The temptation had to do with the lust of the flesh, the lust of the eyes, and the boastful pride of life. God offers to help us in this temptable squeeze (Heb. 4:14-16; I John 1:9; 2:1). But the emphasis in James 1:13-14 is that the cause of man's temptation to do evil is not God, but rather man himself. The heart of man produces all kinds of evil (Rom. 3:10-18; chap. 7; Gal. 5:17-21; Rev. 21:8; Jer. 17:9; Matt. 12:33-35; 15:18-19; I Cor. 6:9-10). Obviously then, it is not always true that "the devil made me do it." We have a formidable foe in our own sin natures! Someone has said, "We have the *world* that's *external*, the *flesh* that's *internal*, and the *devil* that's *infernal*," to deal with every day of our lives!" (Curtis Mitchell). This brings us to:

B. The CULMINATION of Sin, 1:15. The illustration of the culmination of sin's issuing in death is compared to the birth of a child in verse 15. Temptation in and of itself is not sin since it is said of Christ that He "has been tempted in all things as we are, yet without sin" (Heb. 4:15). However, temptation does become sin when we yield to it and obey its bidding. Therefore, we must recognize sin for what it is—an alienator from God and His goodness (Rom. 3:10-18, 23).

We all like things to run smoothly and we are at ease when circumstances are pleasant. Yet life is not like that at all. If evil cravings are allowed to finish their course then dire results will issue. This is most aptly illustrated by the process of gestation. The relationship between the earliest origin of sin and its eventual outcome is pictured in verses 14 and 15. Note the analogy provided by Dr. James E. Rosscup.

PROCESS OF GESTATION Involving a Child	PROCESS OF TEMPTATION Involving Sin
1. Attraction—of a woman to a man ("carried away")	1. Attraction—of the old sin nature to something.
2. Enticement—a woman's desire for sexual intimacies with a man is aroused ("enticed")	2. Enticement to sin
3. Conception—the embryo begins to exist ("conceived"). Hidden but real.	3. The conception of sin within.
4. Birth of a child—("it gives birth to"). The child emerges in visible form.	4. The birth of sin—it comes out into the open and is seen in some recognizable way.
5. Growth and then process of deterioration ("accomplished"). The Greek Aorist Passive means "when it has reached full stature," and could depict a child's growth to the peak of manhood, before the slow tendency toward old age and death.	5. Process of sin resulting in enjoyment which is an illusion.
6. Death	6. Death

C. The CONSEQUENCES of Sin, 1:15. Temptation comes. We toy with the possibility and entertain the thought (Ps. 66:18). Then we commit the act and lust conceives. "They conceive mischief, and bring forth iniquity" (Isa. 59:4). This conception, in turn, "gives birth to sin; and when sin is accomplished," connoting the reaching of full stature or measure, "it brings forth death." Death is what sin brings into being. Therefore the consequences of sin is death—"the wages of sin is death" (Rom. 6:23).

The death here can mean physical death in some instances as well as a deadening of interest in the things of God. Believers can sometimes be disciplined by God through physical death. Yes, sin that is allowed to progress and grow can finally result in death as a chastisement from God (I John 5:16-20; I Cor. 5:1-5; 11:17, 30; Acts 5:10; and Lev. 10:1-2). Lehman Strauss warns, "Let a man weigh the pleasures of sin, which are but for a season, with an endless eternity to regret, remorse, and the bitter agonies of divine retribution, and he will make the wise choice to stand with Jesus Christ and the people of God. Before you sin, weigh the recompense of the reward for sin (Heb. 11:26)."

D. The CONCERN We Need, 1:16. The words of James are pointed. "Do not be deceived...." The term "deceived" (*planasthe*) is where we derive our English word "planet." A planet is a wandering body. When a man is deceived he is caused to wander in his mind. James is concerned that these Jewish Christians would deceive themselves to think that temptation and sin and death come from God.

"My beloved brethren" is the endearing term by which James refers to these of the *diaspora*. Those who were scattered after the stoning of Stephen and the subsequent persecution mentioned in Acts 7–8:3. At least 16 times he addresses them as "brethren." Not only were they both Jewish but they were also bound together in the like precious faith of the lovely Lord Jesus Christ.

For sure, God hates the *sin*, but loves the *sinner* (John 3:16; Rom. 5:8). If a brother wanders, God still loves him. Remember the parable of the prodigal son in Luke 15:11-32? What a rascal he was, but daily his father looked for him "a long way off" (15:20). And when his son returned home his father "felt compassion for him, and ran and embraced him, and kissed him" (15:20). God's attitude toward a wandering one who returns home is expressed in these words: "But we had to be merry and rejoice, for this brother of yours was dead and has begun to live, and was lost and has been found" (15:32).

II. THE RECOGNITION OF GOD AND HIS GIFTS, 1:17-18

After the writer has absolved God of all responsibility to solicit man to do evil, he makes a tremendous statement. He says, "Every good thing bestowed and every perfect gift is from above, coming down from the Father of lights, with whom there is no variation, or shifting shadow" (1:17). "Every good thing bestowed" is the translation of the Greek word *dosis* which denotes the act of giving. In its original sense this means "to give, to present, with the implied idea of giving freely. James wants us here to have a glimpse into the character of God" (Zodiates). But before we contemplate God's character we need to see:

A. The CHARACTERISTICS of God's Gifts, 1:17. His gifts are good, bestowed and perfect. They are from above not from *within* man, where resides the origin of lust. The word "above" (*anothen*) is the same word used in John 3:3, "...unless one is born again (Lit. "from above"), he cannot see the kingdom of God."

James is clearly describing the characteristics of God's gifts to inform his readers that they,

> rather than foolishly *implicating* His gifts, realizing He is good, they should set aside an attitude of accusation and rejection for one of appropriation and receptivity (v. 21). In response to testings, men often are tempted into sin, and can see that the answer to life is not in their undesirable selves, but only in God and His desirable gifts. The man who knows the character of God and is receptive toward Him is able to meet testings and temptations triumphantly (Ross-cup).

Since some of these Jewish converts to Christ were contending that temptation originated in God, James was very concerned that they knew for a fact that the Lord was the source of everything that is good. Even the pagan is able to enjoy the good things of a world which is made by God. The Lord Jesus remarked on the benevolence of God's gifts even to the man without God. This is recorded in Matthew 5:45: "...for He causes His sun to rise on the evil and the good, and sends rain on the righteous and the unrighteous." Every gift that God sends is good and everything that God creates is good. If it comes from God, it is good (Mal. 3:6: Matt. 19:17).

B. The CHARACTER of God Himself, 1:17. After identifying the characteristics of God's gifts, James relates their source as "coming down from the Father of lights, with whom there is no variation, or shifting shadow" (1:17). "The Father of lights" is a descriptive term which denotes the creative activity of God.

"Lights" refer to the heavenly lumineries like the sun, moon and stars (Gen. 1:14). "James is evidently using the heavenly bodies as the most fitting examples of God's gifts which illustrate the point that God's character is *light* in contrast to evil. He is thinking of a proper analogy between physical light which God made and spiritual light which He is" (Rosscup). John says that in Him is no darkness at all (I John 1:5). The word "of" reveals His creative source. Again we see that this Great *God* is a Great

Giver. He is the source and origin of good gifts. It is said of Papillion, when he was confined in the penal colony of French Ghianah, that he was continually gazing off across the water to where freedom could be found. Time and again he would attempt escape, and time and again he would be apprehended. Papillion derived pleasure just in the anticipation of being free. With the Lord, it is different. It is not just the anticipation but the reality that He is a Great Giver and He gives enough. Paul put it this way, "But I have received everything in full...I am amply supplied..." (Phil. 4:18). The words "coming down" should be understood as God's continuing to bestow good things in abundance.

The remainder of verse 17 is most instructive:"...whom there is no variation, or shifting shadow." Simply stated God does not change. He is completely consistent. The writer to the Hebrews reinforces this by stating, "Jesus Christ is the same yesterday and today, yes and forever" (Heb. 13:8). Therefore, we cannot attribute to Him, the sin which springs from ourselves. As Alfred Plummer says, "There is never a time at which one could say that through momentary diminition in holiness it had become a tempter."

C. His COMPASSION in Salvation, 1:18. In this great verse James brings to a head his argumentation that God is not the source of temptation. Previously he demonstrated that for God to be the originator of evil cravings is diametrically opposed to His very essence or nature (1:13) and to His constant goodness (1:17). Now he appeals to his readers' experiences in and God's work of regeneration. Mayor gives the nitty gritty of this verse: "So far from God's tempting us to evil, His will is the cause of our regenration."

1. The POWER of Regeneration, 1:18. Verse 18 sounds almost like Paul penned it (cf. Rom. 8:28-30; 9:14-24; Eph. 1:3-14). The discussion is the sovereign will of God. James is saying that "God's supreme gift to men— adoption into his family, new birth through the Gospel—was no accident" (R.R. Williams).

The Greek New Testament has two words translated by the one English term "will." This "will" is a strong deliberate action. It appears in the simple past tense which relates that the will of God was determined once for all. His will was exercised to provide salvation for a lost humanity in a definite point in time (Luke 19:10). When this was done and the church was conceived, even "the gates of Hades shall not overpower it" (Matt. 16:18). There is nothing that can prevail against the soverign will of God (Rom. 8:31-39).

This is a beautiful truth for God to will such a marvelous salvation brought about by regeneration. Regeneration has many facets like a diamond, each to be understood and appreciated:

a. Regeneration means new birth or re-creation (Titus 3:5).

b. Redemption means to buy out of the marketplace of sin and death (Gal. 3:3).

c. Justification is "to declare righteous" (Rom. 3:24-31).

d. Sanctification connotes being set apart for God (Phil. 1:1).

e. Repentance means "to change the mind" (Acts 17:30; II Cor 7:8-11; Matt. 21:28-29).

f. Faith is the belief in the God of the Bible and in Jesus Christ who came into this world, and the adherence in and cleaving to Christ as Lord and Saviour (John 1:12; James 2:14-26; Rom. 4:5, 23-25; 5:1).

It is through the exercise of His sovereign will that salvation, with all of the above attendant features, is accomplished.

The word "by" in verse 18 demonstrates quite clearly the instrument employed in the new birth. It is "the word of truth." This is none other than the Word of God (I Peter 1:23), the Bible with its gospel message (II Cor. 6:7; Col. 1:5; Eph 1:13; II Tim. 2:15). How important is the Bible? God esteems it pretty high for we read in the Psalms that God has magnified His Word above His name (138:2 New Scofield). How high do we regard the Word of Truth? "For the Word of God is living and active and sharper than any two-edged sword, and piercing as far as the division of soul and spirit, of both joints and marrow, and able to judge the thoughts and intentions of the heart" (Heb. 4:12). Absolutely, the Scriptures are the instrument of eternal life. John elucidates, "No one who is born of God practices sin, because His seed abides in him; and he cannot sin, because he is born of God" (I John 3:9). This is God's regeneration of us accomplished through His Word.

The Father was the *planner* of regeneration (Eph. 1:3-6). The Son was the *provider* of regeneration (John 5:24; Rom. 10:17). May I say to you, dear reader, that I am a preacher of the Word of God. I know its power and I have seen it work. It changes lives, gives hope, and brings forth the new birth. When I am disheartened, down, discouraged or depressed, I give myself the same spiritual prescription that I give to others—a big dose of the Bible. It is the pause that refreshes! It is finding help fast in the Bible pages! Isaiah recorded it well: "So shall My word be which goes forth from My mouth; it shall not return to Me empty, without accomplishing what I desire, and without succeeding in the matter for which I sent it" (55:11). It is God's *will*, accomplishing God's *work*, in God's *way*, by means of God's *Word*!

2. The PURPOSE of Regeneration, 1:18. The clause "that we might be as it were the first fruits among His creatures" reveals the purpose of God's power in regeneration. The word "first fruits" implies more to come. The term dates back to the Old Testament. G. Coleman Luck observes, "The first sheaf of the new crop, together with a sacrifice, was presented in the Levitical ceremony in the temple on the day after the Passover Sabbath. By this, acknowledgment was made that all came from God and belonged to Him, and none was to be used for food until this ceremony had been performed." We must remember that James is writing to Israelis who had been brought to Christ in the Acts 1-7 period. These became the "first fruits" from all nations as the Gospel spread like a prairie fire. Rosscup believes that "Israel was the 'first fruit' of God's increase in Old Testament times (Jer. 2:3), standing before God in a relationship unique among nations (Amos 3:2; Exod. 4:22; Jer. 31:9)." Israelis became the "first fruits" of James 1:18 because they were a guarantee of many more converts to come; namely, Gentiles (Matt. 10:5-7; Luke 24:47-48; Acts 1:8; and Rom. 9,10, and 11). Therefore the purpose of regeneration is to produce "first fruits." These are those whom God owns (Lev. 23:9-14; Deut. 26:1-2) since He has bought them with a price (I Cor. 6:19-20). They are the New Testament Christians bought and paid for by the blood of Jesus Christ (Heb. 9:11-15; 13:10-14; Rev. 1:5).

III. THE RESULT OF REGENERATION, 1:19

The result of regeneration is a changed life (James 2:17; II Cor. 5:17; I John 1:6; 2:6, 11, 19; 3:6-10). Tasker reinforces this with,

> Because God is the originator of the new birth, the characteristics of the new life which that birth inaugurates must be obedience to God, and a readiness to listen to His Word as it is found in the records of His revealed will in Scripture and in what He may speak to His children through the voice of conscience.

Even John postulates an evidence that the life of God is in the believer when he emulates God's character and keeps His commandments (I John 2:3-5).

The statement: "this you know, my beloved brethren" reminds them that they are definitely aware of the heavenly source of their regeneration (new birth). Therefore, they were to be sure that their life style magnified the indwelling Christ. "But let every one be quick to hear, slow to speak and slow to anger!" This does not have primary reference to speech in general, as in the Book of Proverbs, where there are so many great guidelines to govern the mouth (Prov. 10:19; 13:3; 17:28; 29:20). The context clues us in that it refers to the Word of God. In other words, listen to God's Word. Ross warns: "Ceaseless talkers may easily degenerate into fierce controversialists, and may indulge in wild denunciations of those who oppose them, denunciations in which they may sometimes fancy they are doing God service, but which really do more harm than good." Yes, the people of our churches should listen to the Word of God and not the torrential twaddle which emits from the mouth of a dissident gossiper.

Yet, there is a morbid curiosity that draws many to the gossipers of the church. Some people thrive on this degenerate activity. That is why the Scriptures forbid a woman who gossips to be a deaconess in the church. I Timothy 3:11 presents the qualifications for a deaconess as "...dignified, not malicious gossips, but temperate, faithful in all things." The words "malicious gossips" describe one who is given to faultfinding with the demeanor and conduct of others, and spreading innuendos and criticisms. The noun form is used as a name for the devil, who slanders and accuses God; thus, the deaconess must not be a "she-devil" who gossips. Dear friend, do not listen to females or males who practice the satanic function of gossiping. Listen only to those who teach the Word of God and live in the good of it; because listening to the Word of God and being slow to gossip are the results of one who is born again.

IV. THE RECEPTION OF THE WORD OF GOD, 1:20

Verse 19 has noted the results of being born again. One of those results was not listening to gossipers, who produce anger, but a receptivity to God's Word, which produces a life style comparable to Christ. This reception of the Word of God is not characterized by anger.

Is anger ever justified for the believer? Ephesians 4:26 says, "Be angry, and yet do not sin; do not let the sun go down upon your anger." John records that Christ made a scourge of cords with which He literally drove the money-changers from the Temple and overturned their tables (John 2:14-17). Well, is it ever OK to be angry? I feel there are two questions that need to be answered first. One, where is the source of anger? Two, why is one angry?

Question Number One: The one who hears and practices God's Word will evidence self-control at all times (Gal. 5:22-26). Christ was always controlled by the Holy Spirit, and we have already noted that no temptation ever came from *within* Christ, always from *without*. When you and I get angry, is it our own selfish hearts that are making us angry?

Question Number Two: What is the cause of the anger? To be angry at sin is justified. "Hate evil, you who love the Lord" (Ps. 97:10). The Ephesians 4:26 passage indicates that "a believer can be angry apart from sinning. If I am angry at nothing but sin, I can be angry so as not to sin" (Strauss).

Strauss also gives a warning:

> Now we must beware lest we excuse sheer temper by calling it righteous indignation. If a violent passion is aroused in my mind, accompanied by the desire to take vengeance or to obtain satisfaction from one who has offended me, and that passion is accompanied by a hidden malice or smouldering resentment in my heart, I have sinned.

As Proverbs 19:19 states, "A man of great anger shall bear the penalty." The Bible condemns the loss of temper or sinful anger (Matt. 5:22, Gal. 5:20, Eph. 4:31). The words of Proverbs are instructive again: "A gentle answer turns away wrath, but a harsh word stirs up anger" (15:1). All of us, therefore, must not let righteous indignation continue too long, or else it will become uncontrolled anger.

James outlines why the Christian must be slow to anger because it "does not achieve the righteousness of God." In other words, anger does nothing but retard one's testimony for God. The righteous character of God does not fly off the handle. In the words of Paul, "But I say, walk by the Spirit, and you will not carry out the desire of the flesh" (Gal. 5:16).

Words
Are
Cheap

THE CHAPTER OUTLINED:

Words come easy and words are cheap. A brother or sister may say that he or she loves the Lord Jesus; but, does the life reflect the profession? It is easy to profess that one is a Christian. But the fundamental issue is whether or not one's life style is in conformity to the Person of Christ. The purpose of this chapter is to "prove yourselves doers of the word, and not merely hearers who delude themselves" (James 1:22).

I. THE PROCEDURE IN RECEIVING THE WORD, 1:21

Wessell captures the thrust of verse 21 when he writes, "Since the Word is a seed, it must have good soil in which to thrive." Back in verse 19 James exhorted his readers to be quick to hear the Word of the Lord and slow to speak one's own opinion (or even to hear the non-Biblical opinions of the gossipers). Here in verse 21 he is sharing *how* his readers are to receive the precious Word. Simply put, their receptivity was to be characterized by "putting aside all filthiness and all that remains of wickedness, in humility receive the word implanted, which is able to save your souls."

The first word of verse 21 is "Therefore." It connects the principle of thought concerning the Word of Truth (1:18) and *how* it must govern the life and *how* it is to be received (1:21). Through the instrumentality of His Word, God brought us forth out of the sphere of death into the realm of His very own life. Also, by the instrumentality of His Word we are to live our new life in Christ.

As Strauss aptly observes:

The Bible is the only safe and sensible standard of right and wrong. Its precepts do not take the joy out of life; they make life worth living. To the believer in Jesus Christ the Word of God is "the perfect law of liberty," not a code of "Do's and Don'ts."

The concept of governing one's conduct by a list of stringent regulations is "legalism." There is no Biblical foundation for it, therefore it is untenable. As a matter of fact, it is rankingly unbiblical! Yet, some contemporary Christians maintain a mentality controlled by codified Christian conduct. This is very similar to the problem that was prevalent in the Galatian epistle. Paul was very harsh with these first century legalists. He said, "You foolish Galatians, who has bewitched you..." (Gal. 3:1). The word foolish means "no understanding." Certainly the legalist is without understanding as to the real meaning of spirituality.

Legalism was the modus operandi of the Pharisees. They had 613 rules which they were bound to follow daily. These were Talmudic regulations built around the Law of Moses and the Mishnah (codified scribal law). Permit me to share some of these with you as examples of the absurdity of legalism.

If a person's chicken laid an egg on the Sabbath, he could not eat that egg. If he did eat the egg, he must kill that chicken on the next day, since the chicken violated the Sabbath. Laying an egg was work, even for a chicken, and no work was permitted on the Sabbath, which included hens.

The Talmud goes on and on as to what one could and could not do. The rules, regulations and evasions piled up ad infinitum to the ridiculous. Take another case as an example, that of carrying a burden. One could not bear a burden on the Sabbath; but, a burden needed to be defined. It was defined as "food equal in weight to a dried fig, enough wine for mixing in a goblet, milk enough to put upon a wound, oil enough to anoint a small member, water enough to moisten an eye-salve," and so forth. Such weighty matters had to be resolved whether or not a woman could wear a brooch, a man could wear a wooden leg or dentures on the Sabbath; or would it be carrying a burden to do so? Could a chair or even a child be lifted? On and on went the legalistic hassles.

Dear reader, the only difference between the Pharisees then and some Christians now is that the do's and don'ts are different. The basic approach is the same. Whether the list is five ("The Filthy Five") or nine ("The Nasty Nine") or twelve ("The Dirty Dozen") it remains legalism and that is gross in the eyes of God.

I am reminded of a popular camp song in the 60s which had the following: "We are the boys in blue; we don't smoke and we don't chew and we don't go with the girls that do." If negativism is the evidence of a spiritual Christian, then my dog is a good Christian because she doesn't smoke or chew either. No, my friend, the dynamic of Christ is not a legal orientation, but a love orientation. If we love Him, we want to receive His Word in all of its positive glory (Ps. 42:1; John 13:34-35; 15:10; I John 2:3). Keeping His commandments is not loving Him; but, loving Him is keeping his commandments! These are not the artificial commandments of men with all of their superficiality! They are the words of God which flow through a life that is rightly related to the Lord.

As James says, "Putting aside all filthiness...." *Legalism*, which is an inadequate answer to sin, is very bad. But, just as bad is *license*, which is permissive attitude toward sin. The believer must recognize sin for what it is. He can't just ignore it and hope that it will go away—he must *put* it aside!

Sin is not a mistake or a human frailty to be excused or a psychological hang-up, it is "filthiness." There is a tendency today to gloss over sin, and some liberal preachers have attempted to lower even the wages of sin. But the wages are still *death* (Rom. 6:23)! Before even a Christian can receive the Word of God, there must be a certain procedure to follow. That procedure is simply to "lighten up." He must lighten himself of certain encumbrances (Heb. 12:1-2).

Verse 21 is a conditional sentence in the Greek text. In other words, if the believer lays apart all that is filthy, then he will be able to receive the Word of God which keeps his soul safe.

Looking at some key words is important. The phrase "Putting aside" reveals that when Christ comes into a life, a real battle ensues between the old sin nature and the new nature in Christ (Rom. 8:5-9). Therefore the trappings of the old life need to be stripped away (Eph. 4:22-25; Col. 3:5; Rom, 13:12; I Peter 2:1). "The word is used of clothes, but also of the removal of dirt from the body..." (Ropes). As one would take off a garment, as an act of the will, he is to put off the evil habits and propensities to do evil which James calls "filthiness."

The word "filthiness" is most meaningful to the Christian reader. Zodiates is "right on" when he says that "filth, strictly speaking is used of wax in the ear." Sin is like wax in the ear; it hinders God's Word from entering the brain. But the dimension of sin in some Christians' lives is more like a banana in the ear than wax. Remove the banana (I John 1:9), brother and sister, which keeps you from hearing and doing (practicing) the Word of Truth.

James also tells us to put aside "all that remains of wickedness" or literally "abundance of malice." R. J. Knowling notes that "in classical Greek the word translated 'malice' is often used for vice in general...." I believe this should be the idea here.

The procedure is "in humility receive the word implanted...." The receptive attitude of the hearer is to be surrounded by and enveloped "in humility." Obviously, this is "opposed to malice" (Marvin R. Vincent). We are to humble ourselves before the Word of God and a malicious disposition cannot do that. Henry Jacobsen gives this illustration:

> Mark Twain, who was not a believer, said he had no problem with parts of the Bible that he couldn't understand. The parts that gave him trouble, he said, were those that he understood all too well. You, too, will find that your problem is not with your inability to understand Scripture—it is with your unwillingness to live by the parts that are perfectly clear to you.

Receive the word in humility, being willing to obey and change when it says to change. Do not resist its conviction as do the malicious. It is very profitable to receive His Truth—"And those are the ones on whom seed was sown on the good ground; and they hear the word and accept it, and bear fruit, thirty, sixty, and a hundredfold" (Mark 4:20).

James' use of the word "receive" is significant. Just as one was to put aside, in a point in time, all sin, so he is to receive, in a point in time, the Word. "Receive" also appears in the mood of command which means that for the believer to not "in humility receive the word" is disobedience and disobedience is sin. "Receive" carries the idea of putting out the welcome mat for the Word of God in a personal manner (Acts 17:11; I Thess. 1:6; 2:13).

Notice that the word is "implanted." "James goes to the realm of horticulture for a vivid picture of the relationship the Word sustains to the believer. His idea is that a plant of God within the life grows out and manifests the realities of faith in foliage and fruit" (Rosscup). Needless to say there are other Scriptures which compare the Christian to a tree or a vine bringing forth fruit (Ps. 1: Jer. 17:6-8; John 15; James 3:12). A. T. Robertson adds, "The figure is that of the seed sown in the heart and taking root and growing there. So Jesus spoke of the man who had no root in himself (Matt. 13:21)."

James concludes verse 21 by stating what the Word of Truth can do; namely, "which is able to save your souls." Remember that James is writing to those who are already born again (Hebrew Christians that are scattered). Therefore, he is not arguing that they receive the Word in order to gain salvation—they have already done that. He refers to them as "brethren" at least 16 times. Yet, in one sense, they were to grow in the Word "in respect to salvation" (I Peter 1:5, 9, 13, 2:2). But there is another sense to what James is saying here. The correct understanding of James' thought is in the word "save" (*sozo*). It can mean more than deliverance from hell as Abbott-Smith relates: "To save from peril, injury of suffering...of healing, restoring to health." I believe that James means that their souls will be "kept safe" (Thayer). This is thrilling! Fellow Christian, if we want to guard our "souls", we always must welcome His Word in a humble and submissive manner. "Souls" is to be understood in the full sense, that of the whole life. "As long as we are on the earth, our souls will need the healing and saving power of the living Word of God, Jesus, who comes to us through the written Word of God, the Bible" (Downey).

II. THE PROOF THAT THE WORD IS RECEIVED, 1:22

Where this action is determines whether or not someone is a genuine believer. If his action is in the realm of the world, the flesh and the devil, then he is not the Lord's. If his action is in the area of the Word of God, then he is the Lord's. With common concession, a doer of the Word "backs-up" his life and proves that he has received the Word and lives in the good of it.

"But prove yourselves" is a much too elaborate translation of the original Greek. Christianity is a faith that works. It is a belief that produces action. The concept conveyed in the above phrase is simply, "But keep on becoming" (Robertson). The writer has already informed the readers of the importance of listening to the Word of God (1:19). Hearing the Word only is not sufficient. Doing is the natural proof or demonstration of one's listening when He said, "...My mother and My brothers are those who hear the word of God and do it" (Luke 8:21). Friends, our churches are filled with spiritual *sponges* who *soak* up the information. We need to put into practice what we hear from the Word of God.

Perhaps James had in mind once again the legalists like the external-oriented, ceremonial-conscious Pharisees. They were empty of content. In Matthew 23, Jesus blasted their hypocrisy in one of the most scathing oratories in the history of man. In Matthew 7:24-27 we find the following contrast:

> Therefore every one who hears these words of Mine, and acts upon them, may be compared to a wise man, who built his house upon the rock; and the rain descended, and the floods came, and the winds blew, and burst against that house; and yet it did not fall; for it had been founded upon the rock. And every one who hears these words of Mine, and does not act upon them, will be like a foolish man, who built his house upon the sand. And the rain descended, and the floods came, and the winds blew, and burst against that house; and it fell, and great was its fall.

Those who merely hear the Word of God "delude themselves." There is nothing worse than self-deception or self-delusion. "Hearers" was used in the ancient world for auditors. Auditors do not take tests, nor do they get degrees, awards or diplomas. The Word of God needs to penetrate the life so that one becomes a doer.

"Doers of the word" (*poietai logou*) is the source of our English word "poet." A poet is one who puts words together in a beautiful and meaningful manner. A doer of the Word is one who makes beauty and harmony with God. Let us all be doers and not simply auditors.

Think of Jesus, beloved. What a doer he was. His life was characterized by tireless and ceaseless activity. "He healed all manner of diseases. Something happened wherever He went: people were transformed, homes were changed, a new spirit appeared in the marketplace, women were lifted to a high estate and children, loved as never before, became the patterns of the Kingdom" (Louis H. Evans).

Jesus is our example of hard work and doing. Jesus also has a promise for us, "...blessed are those who hear the word of God, and observe it" (Luke 11:28). Doing is backing-up your life.

III. THE PATTERN OF DOING, 1:23-27

Obviously, there needs to be a change in the lives of the hearers, not simple acquiescence that it was truth spoken. This change is evidenced in becoming a doer of the Word. It is tragic when one hears the Word of God and he is not a doer. But, James draws an analogy in verses 23 through 25 to assist his readers in determining whether or not they are doers.

A. An ANALOGY for Doing, 1:23-25. James sets up an analogy so that these Hebrew brethren might know what is really involved in doing the Word. James speaks of a mirror and says there are two ways one might look into it. He contrasts this to two ways one may look into the Great Book of God.

1. The Tragedy of the Casual Glance, 1:23-24. Mirrors don't lie. A normal mirror will reveal a natural reflection. When a man looks into a mirror, he beholds his "natural face." This literally is "the face of his birth"; in other words, the face with which he was born. The glass mirrors his exact appearance. The Bible is a lot like that mirror, for it perfectly portrays the condition of the heart (the one with which he was born). The hearing-but-not-doing man is described in verse 23 "for once he has looked at himself and gone away, he has immediately forgotten what kind of person he was." Phillips paraphrases this verse in the following: "He sees himself, it is true, but he goes on with whatever he is doing without the slightest recollection of what sort of person he saw in the mirror."

Looking into the Scriptures should not be casual. We should never forget what we see in the Book. It can change our lives. "How can a young man keep his way pure? By keeping it according to Thy word....Thy word I have treasured in my heart, that I may not sin against Thee" (Ps. 119:9,11). The Word should improve our spiritual appearance.

2. The Transformation of the Careful Gaze, 1:25. Needless to say that the careful gaze is diametrically opposed to the casual glance in that the former *transforms* the life and the latter is *tragic*. The one who studies

God's Word with the full purpose of changing his behavior patterns is described by the human author as "one who looks intently at the perfect law...." Verse 25 is certainly in contradistinction to verse 24 as is noted by the word "but." This is a strong word of contrast in the original Greek language of the New Testament. The mirror of the previous two verses (1:23-24) reflects the physical appearance, whereas the perfect law reveals the personality of the heart, the condition of the inner core.

The "perfect law" is another way of saying the Word of God or the Word of Truth (1:18) or the gospel of grace (Gal. 6:12; Rom. 12:2). The Psalmist says: "The law of the Lord is perfect, restoring the soul; the testimony of the Lord is sure making wise the simple" (Ps. 19:7)!

The Word is also denoted as "the law of liberty." This phrase explains why the law is perfect because it "rests on the work of Christ, whose truth sets us free" (John 8:32; II Cor. 3:16; Rom. 8:2). The word rendered "liberty" appears 11 times in the New Testament. The Cambridge Greek Testament elucidates:

> The freedom of the law of Christ is contrasted with the bondage to minute precepts which characterized the developed Mosaic system ...Galatians 5:1; John 8:32; Romans 8:5....The law of Christ then is called a perfect law because it is final and complete, as distinct from the Mosaic law, which was transitory and imperfect; it is called a law of liberty because it is the expression of a Father's love for his children, not for a Master's law for slaves.

Wordsworth's Greek Testament gives these encouraging words:

> Christ has redeemed us by His blood from the slavery of sin and Satan into the glorious liberty of the Sons of God....He has redeemed us from the curse of the law (Gal. 3:13), and purchased us to Himself (I Cor. 6:20; 7:23), and has thus made us free (John 8:36), and has conveyed to us these blessings effected by the operation of the Holy Ghost, which is therefore called God's free Spirit (Ps. 51:12; II Cor. 3:17); and has revealed to us these things in the preaching of the Gospel, which is the perfect Law of Liberty, the Law of emancipation from evil, and of obedience to God, whose service is perfect freedom, and has bound us to obey the Law of love, and to serve one another thereby (Gal. 5:13) as servants of God (I Peter 2:16). So that while we are free by faith, we must all serve by love. And let him take heed to obey his law of liberty, for by it he will be judged (James 2:12).

James, you will recall, is a Jew who is writing to Jews. They were familiar with the Old Testament described as the "law." It was Christ who made this law perfect for the New Testament is in the Old *concealed* and the Old Testament is in the New *revealed*. Therefore as they read the Scriptures, they were to take a careful gaze into the "Mirror of God." Christ Himself said, "If you know these things, you are blessed if you do them" (John 13:17). As the reader obeys and submits to the Word, then greater understanding becomes his portion. "Then He opened their minds to understand the Scriptures" (Luke 24:45). The Lord sends His Holy Spirit to open hearts when the Word of God is opened by hearing and doing (John 16:13-15).

Praise the Lord! The doer of the Word is free. In the words of C. Leslie Mitton, "This obedience to God is a wonderful freedom ('His service is perfect freedom'), and this freedom of the child of God is freedom to do what most we love doing—pleasing God."

This is practical truth. This scratches where you and I itch. James is like that. He doesn't deal in "Disneyland" doctrine. He tells it just like it is! James is exciting, stimulating and thrilling. He gets down where we live and move and have our being. James candidly conveys the concepts of Christ to his contemporaries and it grabs us hard. Yes, the truth of the Book of James is practical as it moves on the highway of life where the rubber meets the road. James is not only concerned with the *content* of one's belief, but also the *character* of his behavior. Be a doer of the Word! That is practical! Back up your life in the game of life by what you do, and look like it! The popular preacher, Charles Spurgeon, was admonishing a class of divinity students on the importance of making the facial expressions harmonize with the speech in delivering sermons. "When you speak of heaven," he said, "let your face light up and be irradiated with a heavenly gleam. Let your eyes shine with reflected glory. And when you speak of hell...well, then your everyday face will do."

B. The ACTIONS of an Empty Profession, 1:26. Self-deception is an ever-present threat to the people who want to serve the Lord. James wants to compare two religious persons in order to warn his readers of the dangers of delusion. On one hand, James discusses the professor who does not practice and studies his actions of empty profession (1:26). On the other hand, he depicts the professor who practices and surveys his activities of indwelling possession (1:27). First of all, notice the following two things about empty profession, 1:26.

1. The essence of his religion is seen in that he professes to be religious, and in the words of James: "thinks himself to be religious." Religion is the practice of external forms, ceremonies and observances. It is legalistic codification of conduct. It is a form of godliness, although the internal power is denied (II Tim. 3:5). A legalist was no nearer the kingdom of heaven than a murderer; but, one couldn't convince him of that. The Pharisees were the leading exponents of religion. As a matter of fact, they were the hyper-legalists. They were extremely hung-up on the law. I do not necessarily mean the Mosaic Law, but all kinds of oral laws. Every-time a Rabbi stated a principle, they made it a law.

The religious man in James has deceived his own heart in that he undertakes indefatigable, external duties to please God. This man was programmed for law and works. He needed to know that a genuine doer of the Word performed because of the result of the indwelling Holy Spirit. True religion is an inside-out job and *never* is the heart affected by an outside-inside job! Never!

The legalist wasn't all wrapped up in religion for exercise. He wanted to get to God. The legalist was a man like Nicodemus in John, chapter 3. I wonder what this dear old man thought when the young Rabbi from Nazareth, Jesus Christ, told him that he had to start all over again. He had lived his life all wrong in a negative, legalistic, traditional and religious manner. He was passionately seeking the kingdom of God. Religion is a curse! Nicodemus had deceived himself for years in thinking that all the sacrifices, rituals, feasts, tithes, ceremonial cleansings, and observances would bring him to God. But Jesus said to poor Nicodemus that he had better scrap the whole thing and begin again. Nicodemus, "You must be born again" (John 3:7). It is an inside-out job wrought in the heart from above!

> The false religions of the world, including the perverted cults of Christianity, are all demon-inspired. As the prince of this world, Satan, is bent on turning men away from the revealed truth of the one true God and from the salvation He has provided for sinful mankind through His Son, Jesus Christ. This is clearly taught in the Word of God. The Apostle Paul stresses this fact not only in con-nection with idolatry (I Cor. 10:20), but with all the false doctrines, including those of so-called Christian cults (Merrill F. Unger).

I am not a religious person. To call me religious is to insult the pro-vision that Christ gave to me (Rom. 5:8). I am not working my way to heaven by religious externalities (Eph. 2:8-9). I am trusting in Christ (John 14:6) not religion. All the religion in the world has never drawn anyone closer to God. It only gives a false sense of security in one's isolation from God. The devil spends most of his time operating through religion (II Cor. 4:4; Rom. 1:21-32; I Tim. 4:1-2; I John 4:1-6; Rev. 9:20-21). Religion is Satan's dynamo! Jesus told Nicodemus in so many words, "Forget it all; you've got to start from the bottom and be born again." Recall what

Jesus said to some other Pharisees: "You are of your father the devil... whenever he speaks a lie, he speaks from his own nature, for he is a liar, and the father of lies" (John 8:44).

This man of James 1:26 professed to be religious. He was high on "doing." Doing is the *result* of a heart that is rightly related to God. Doing is never the *reason* for a heart being rightly related to God. Therefore, this traditionalist, who prided himself on his negative approach to life and who was intensely religious, failed. We see this in:

2. The example of his religion. His example did not back up his life and profession. Jesus said that "you will know them by their fruits" (Matt. 7:16). Believers are not to judge others (Rom. 14:10) but to be "fruit inspectors" is necessary. The religious man of verse 26 "does not bridle his tongue." "The picture is that of a man putting the bridle in his own mouth, not in that of another" (Robertson). This man "deceives his own heart." Therefore his religion is "worthless", meaning that it is vain, empty of content and therefore results in nothing. That's religion for you— change of conduct but no heart change. That's like penal rehabilitation. Clean up a man's act, release him from prison with the same, unchanged heart.

Here, as Guy King suggests, James deals with a subject that is in every man's mouth—the tongue (1:13, 19; 2:3, 7, 12-13, 16; 4:11, 13; 5:6, 9, 12, and others). John Calvin believes that the religious professor is continually pointing out the defects of others in a lustful effort to put himself in a superior light. This is nothing more than a spiritual slander.

C. The ACTIVITIES of an Energizing Possession, 1:27. Needless to repeat, religion is a satanic curse because it hopes in external activities. But, there is a "pure and undefiled religion." Why is a man a doer of the word? If he is religious, he does it to obtain or earn salvation. If he is a Christian, he does it because he already has salvation. In other words, good works *does not* produce salvation; but, salvation *does* produce good works. Therefore, what James means by pure religion is external deeds, which result from a heart indwelt and possessed by the Holy Spirit, who energizes and produces such acts.

1. The essence of his religion is "pure." "This is not the more apparent purity of going through the motions of religious protocol or do's and don'ts which the Pharisees thought sufficient (Mark 7), but genuine cleanness of motive in one's relationship with God and others" (Rosscup).

Obviously, then the religion of the Pharisees was impure since it was done to gain God's acceptance. When Christ told the notable Nicodemus that he would have to be re-created, it was probably too much for him to handle. He more than likely reflected back and said: "I'm a Jew and it doesn't do me any good; I am also a Pharisee and it does me less good!" Jesus said, "Whoever does not receive the kingdom of God like a child shall not enter it at all" (Luke 18:17). In other words, "Strip off impure religion, go back to the bottom and start all over again!"

On what basis, then, does impure religion become pure religion? Not works; but faith! II Corinthians 5:17 states, "Therefore if any man is in Christ, he is a new creature; the old things passed away; behold, new things have come." That is the business that God is in—making brand new creations. Peter says, "For you have been born again not of seed which is perishable but imperishable, that is, through the living and abiding word of God" (I Peter 1:23). That is what happens when one receives Christ (John 1:12)—new life comes into him. A man needs to be re-constructed from the inside. A doctor cannot cure a man's cancer by painting him. He must get inside and root it out. Therefore, as far as the impure religionist is concerned, there is a new game in town called pure religion!

This pure religion is "undefiled." This adjective is derived from the verb which means "to stain with colors." In other words, this one who possesses new life in Christ is characterized by undefiled Christian service; that is, service without anything that would stain or spoil his life. It is "pure and undefiled" not just before men, who are fruit-inspectors, but "in the sight of our God and Father," who is the fruit evaluator. This fruit is represented in:

2. **The examples of his religion** are compassionate and clean.

a. **He is compassionate** in that he visits "orphans and widows in their distress." In the ancient societies there was no welfare state, unemployment benefits, retirement programs, life insurance payments or any other provision like Social Security for widows and orphans. One who was widowed or orphaned was absolutely destitute. Therefore, if anyone helped meet their needs that was an example of real religion.

Today, there is a tendency for church members to make their pastors do all of the calling on the needy. James tells us that *all* who possess Christ should engage in this type of benevolent activity. The Early Church participated in this benevolent function (Acts 6:1, I Tim. 5:1-16). It is clear that if the services of a pastor are needed that he should be summoned (James 5:14). All believers have this responsibility and should not shirk from it. A very good comparison between shirking one's own father or mother is the practice of Corban found in Mark 7:11 and the neglect of members caring for one another can be made. (For a further treatment of this see my book, *God Has A Better Idea—The Home,* which is also published by BMH Books). That practice of parental neglect intently displeased the Lord Jesus, and asking one man to do all of the work of service also displeases the Lord because it violates His Word.

Every Christian must evidence that Christ lives within by continuous acts of compassion. Ross remarks:

> In contrast to the outwardly religious Pharisee who devoured widows' houses (Mark 12:40), Christians should visit orphans and widows in their affliction in order to point them to Him who is the Father of the fatherless and the judge of the widow (Ps. 68:6). In Old Testament times the fatherless and widows were specially cared for and protected by Jehovah: see Deuteronomy 27:19; Psalms 94:6; Jeremiah 17:6; Malachi 3:5; and so forth."

b. He is clean in that he is "to keep oneself unstained by the world." His motives are pure and he practices what the Scriptures teach on helping the needy. Consider these admonitions from Proverbs: "He who is gracious to a poor man lends to the Lord, and He will repay him for his good deed ...He who shuts his ear to the cry of the poor will also cry himself and not be answered..." (Prov. 19:17; 21:13). Psalm 41:1 reiterates: "How blessed is he who considers the helpless; the Lord will deliver him in a day of trouble." John says, "But whoever has this world's goods, and beholds his brother in need and closes his heart against him, how does the love of God abide in him? Little children, let us not love with word or with tongue, but in deed and truth" (I John 3:17-18).

This one is clean for he keeps himself from the smudges of worldliness (II Cor. 6:14-18). The word for "unstained" means "spotless" (Abbott-Smith). It is used of Christ in I Peter 1:19, "but with precious blood, as of a lamb unblemished and spotless, the blood of Christ." In other words, believers, in the clean acts of compassion, are to be Christ-like.

The Cult
of the Clique

THE CHAPTER OUTLINED:

The practice of cliquishness is destroying the individual Christian and, in turn, his church. Somehow the Christian church has borrowed the "clique concept" from the world and it is eating her alive. When people associate only in a small and exclusive coterie, they alienate and severely damage others who are not part of that set.

Christ is not a clique. Therefore, "My brethren, do not hold your faith in our glorious Lord Jesus Christ with an attitude of personal favoritism" (James 2:1).

The purpose of this lesson is to change cliquishness to that of Christian concern in the welfare of others. Cliques must be unveiled so that each class member knows exactly what it is—a disease!

I. THE PROBLEM OF PREJUDICE, 2:1

Once again, the practicality of the Book of James is strikingly seen. The problem under discussion here is one which the average individual in the average community faces every day. These words are simple and practical for they get down where we are. They explode with relevance. Verse 1 exposes the pounding problem of prejudice with its throbbing pulse which vibrates all of society. And, God help us, prejudice permeates even the Christian church!

Never have I heard anything on the subject of prejudice from a Biblical perspective—not in college, seminary, Bible conferences or in any church where I have attended. Yet, if there was ever a subject which needed God's point of view, it is this one.

In chapter 1, James was discussing Christian conduct. He was writing to Jewish converts who had been dispersed due to their faith in Christ as the Messiah. By far the largest number of the first Christians were poor. This stands to reason since in the first century the majority of the Palestinian peoples were poor. The social divisions among the Jews, generally speaking, were two in number. On the one hand, there was the poor from which Jesus called most of His disciples, like the rough men of the waterfront. Dr. James L. Boyer writes, "...the vast majority of the converts to the Christian faith in the early church period were from the common or lower classes of people. This fact is in accord with the sentiment expressed by our Lord in Matthew 11:25 and elsewhere." William Barclay reiterates:

> Somewhere around the year A.D. 178 Celsus wrote one of the bitterest attacks upon Christianity that was ever written. It was precisely this appeal of Christianity to the common people that he ridiculed. He declared that the Christian point of view was, "Let no cultured person draw near, none wise, none sensible; for all that kind

of thing we count evil; but if any man is ignorant, if any is wanting in sense and culture, if any is a fool let him come boldly." Of the Christians he wrote, "We see them in their own houses, wool dressers, cobblers and fullers, the most uneducated and vulgar persons." He said that the Christians were "like swarms of bats—or ants creeping out of their nests—or frogs holding a symposium around a swamp—or worms in conventicle in a corner of mud."

On the other hand, there was the wealthy aristocracy. Since the days of the Maccabees, the Hasmoneans had dominated the Palestinian society. When Herod the Great came to the throne, the Hasmoneans still retained control of the priesthood. In this position they were the virtual rulers of Judea. They controlled the business traffic which was connected with the temple, and participated in the revenues collected there. Thus this religious group, composed of the families of the priests and rabbis, constituted the wealthy aristocracy of Judaism.

It was this element which categorically and unequivocally rejected the messiahship of Jesus. (There were two recorded exceptions; namely, Nicodemus and Joseph of Arimathea—John 19:38-39). Anyone who followed Christ was expelled from the congregation of Israel and excommunicated from the temple. He was literally "unsynagogued"—John 9:22; 12:42; 16:2. These were simply put out of the life of Israel. The aristocracy did not tolerate Christ and, therefore would not tolerate His followers. You see, these religious leaders thought they knew everything and they just *knew* that Jesus was not the Christ. Therefore, they made life miserable; unbearable for believers!

Needless to say, the poor hated the rich. But, believe it or not, the poor would cater to the rich. They did this, many times, just to survive. I could just see the poor smile sweetly at the rich and in their hearts be cursing their existence.

Remember back in James 1:27 our writer displayed that Christian faith produced such exhibits of conduct as compassion for those in need. In 2:1 he turns to the other side of the coin. A poor brother could selfishly discriminate and manifest special deference toward a rich man because he is wealthy, influential or powerful. Perhaps the poor one intends to "get something out of him." Most probably, however, the playing-up to the rich by the poor was for his own protection (2:6). But, for whatever the reason, it is opportunistic, prejudiced behavior and is sin! This type of thing is:

A. INCONGRUOUS with Faith. Verse 1 labels the recipients of this epistle as "My brethren." Therefore prejudice is a sin which Christians can commit. This is reinforced by the phrase "do not hold your faith in our glorious Lord Jesus Christ"—their faith was in Christ!

The term "your faith" is better rendered "the faith" because of the definite article in the Greek. Such prejudiced conduct is incongruous in the life of one who holds the faith of our Lord Jesus Christ; in other words, "who professes to believe in Jesus Christ as his Lord" (Tasker). The principle of faith is manifested in non-prejudiced activity. Prejudice is also:

B. INCOMPATIBLE with Glory. The words "glorious Lord" connote a Jewish flavor. "The intensely Jewish character of this Epistle makes it reasonably certain that the familiar Jewish conception of the *Shekinah* is what the writer is referring to" (*Expositor's Greek Testament*). The word "Shekinah" is from the Hebrew term meaning "to dwell." It simply denotes the visible glory of the Lord's indwelling in men (Luke 2:9; Acts 7:2; Rom. 9:4; Heb. 9:5). Since this is a reference to God's glory in men, then James is telling these Hebrew believers to hold the faith in their Lord Jesus Christ, the *Shekinah*, the "glory." This shows the deity of Christ since "He is the radiance of His glory..." (Heb. 1:3). Indeed, Christ is God dwelling in human flesh and His "Shekinah" is veiled by that physical body (Heb. 10:20). Therefore to express "an attitude of personal favoritism" would be incompatible to the glorious Lord who dwells in the hearts of His people. Prejudice is also:

C. INCONSISTENT with One's Testimony. The construction "personal favoritism" is one word in the test. It is a compound word made of two words; one which means "face, countenance or appearance"; the other meaning "to receive" in its primary sense, but also denotes "to apprehend by the senses, to understand, to seize with the mind." It conveys the following sense: it is the sin of one who prejudices himself against another with respect to the outward appearance. This prejudiced one has no thought of the intrinsic worth of the rich. It is therefore inconsistent to profess Christ and at the same time show prejudice.

II THE PERIL OF PARTIALITY, 2:2-4

James paints a vivid picture of the peril of partiality and illustrates when its true colors are beheld. This sin, partiality, is particularly portrayed in poor people. James speaks of the usher in the ancient synagogues. The word "assembly" (*sunagogen*) in verse 2 literally means the "synagogue." It was the place where the Jews would come together. Remember that most of the early Christians were Jewish believers at first. They still met in synagogues. When a wealthy, highborn or powerful man would enter the assembly, he would be given preferential treatment as he was seated in a prominent place. Perhaps those in charge of seating desired to advance their own prestige. But, more than likely, the poor were afraid and therefore gave special preference to the rich and powerful man.

A. The APPEARANCES, 2:2. The phrase "for if a man" is a third class condition. The idea is maybe he will or maybe he won't. This implies that the rich did not frequent the Christian meetings of worship too often. But if and when he did, he would be dressed in the most extravagant of clothing.

He would have a "gold ring" or literally be "gold-fingered." Of course, the wearing of gold is not wrong. The point is that in James' day very few would have owned a gold ring. Today, it seems as if everyone has a gold ring. Yet, in those days, it was definitely a distinguishing characteristic of the rich.

This one also "dressed in fine clothes." This would be bright or brilliant clothing (Luke 23:11; Acts 10:30; Rev. 19:14). And it was used by the wealthy Pharisees to denote "the Jewish pretensions to purity and holiness" (John P. Lange). The Pharisees were right on schedule again! Jesus said, "They love the place of honor at banquets, and the chief seats in the synagogues" (Matt. 23:6). Jesus spoke of the bright clothing of the scribes as well: "...Beware of the scribes who like to walk around in long robes, and like respectful greetings in the market places, and chief seats in the synagogues, and places of honor at banquets" (Mark 12:38-39). Is this contemporary? Listen to this dialogue: Wife, "Did you see that hat Mrs. Jones wore to church?" Husband, "No!" Wife, "Did you see the new dress Mrs. Smith had on?" Husband, "No!" Wife, "A lot of good it does you to go to church! You never get anything out of it!"

James continues: "...and there also comes in a poor man in dirty clothes." He is poor. He is the very opposite of the rich (Matt. 19:21). He would be a typical Christian of the first century world, probably a man of meager means and, perhaps, no means at all; indeed, poverty riddles. He is dressed in "dirty clothes" which is a polite translation of "filthy." What would the ushers of your congregation do if a man, who was unkempt and filthy like this would walk into your sanctuary?

Well, ironically enough, something like this did happen in my church. It occurred during our informal Wednesday evening prayer and care service. A Bohemian man blew in out of nowhere and he was a mess. He hadn't shaved in years; his hair had one million frizzies; and he was odoriferous; in other words, he yielded an abominable fragrance. He proceeded to sit down next to one of our highbrow ladies. He scratched his beard and belched. She took one look at him (as well as a whiff) and moved over in the pew all the way to the other end. Midway through our service, he rose and staggered out into the night.

Later the lady said, "I've never been so offended! I could smell the liquor and cigarettes all over that man! I'm so glad he left!" It didn't help my rapport with this lady too much when I countered with, "Well, I'm glad that he came. He heard the Gospel. And I hope he comes back!" I thought she was going to get up and walk out as well. But, on second thought, she wouldn't go out because that awful man was somewhere lurking in the dark with liquor on his breath. Samuel has told us of the Divine Viewpoint when he quoted the Lord: "Do not look at his appearance or at the height of his stature...for God sees not as man sees, for man looks at the outward appearance, but the Lord looks at the heart" (I Sam. 16:7).

B. The ATTITUDE, 2:3. Verse 3 took place two thousand years ago and informs us what some in the Early Church would do when Mr. Moneybags or Mr. Poor would attend. "And you pay special attention to the one who is wearing the fine clothes, and say, 'You sit here in a good place,' and you say to the poor man, 'You stand over there, or sit down by my footstool.'"

The Bible says that God is vitally concerned about every man no matter what His economic station in life (Deut. 1:17; 10:17; Ps. 68:10; Luke 7:16). God is ever-mindful of a man's needs (Matt. 10:30-31). Obviously then, no one is to consider someone else as less or beneath him (Phil. 2:3-4). Someone has well stated, "He who looks down on his neighbor is surely living on a bluff!"

James is the epistle of right living. It contains the rules for the game of life. It presents a practical faith that works.

C. The APPRAISAL, 2:3-4. In verses 3 and 4, it is clearly declared that one who commits the sin of partiality has an erroneous sense of values. Partiality reveals a false value system; namely, appraisal by means of external values. Partiality is a mental sinful attitude which gushes forth from an evil heart. "For as he thinks within himself, so he is..." (Prov. 23:7). Yes, from the heart comes sinful actions (Mark 7:21-23).

The practice of partiality demands an affirmative answer to the rhetorical question of 2:4: "Have you not made distinctions among yourselves." This one is divided in his own mind like the two-souled man of 1:8. Those permeated with partiality have "become judges with evil motives."

III. THE POSITION OF THE POOR, 2:5-7

A. The CHOICE of God, 2:5. Verse 5 sounds like James is on the soap box. He's getting all worked up like a fiery evangelist fanning the revival flames with a passionate appeal. He fires away, "Listen, my beloved brethren."

"Did not God choose" reminds his Jewish readers that they were God's chosen people (Deut. 14:1-2). The Greek word is the root for our English derivative "election." "The Jews had come in many cases to look on earthly prosperity as a mark of divine favor and poverty as a sign of God's disfavor" [cf. Ps. 73] (Robertson). There are some church board members today who believe the reverse of the above. They espouse that a poor preacher is a good preacher. They attempt to keep him humble by underpaying the poor man. This is nothing more than a "sanctimonious salary syndrome." The tradition of equating poverty and piety is bad news! Frankly, I never want to be afflicted with either plague. Poverty is a rebuke to my Lord's provisions for His own and piety is a pathetic substitute for vibrant spirituality. "There is no special virtue in poverty itself, and sometimes it is the result of slothfulness" [Prov. 24:30-34] (Rosscup). But the lust for wealth is just as bad.

The Pharisees were lovers of money (Luke 16:14). This is wrong as well (I Tim. 6:10-11). "But the troubles of the Jews, in spite of many wealthy Pharisees and Sadducees, had led many of them to see a blessing in poverty" (Robertson). James says that "God chose the poor of this world to be rich in faith!" "Rich in faith" means they were rich because of their faith. "James does not affirm that God chose all the poor people" (Matt. 10:23-26; I Cor. 1:26-28) (Robertson). James has reference to the words of Jesus when He gave the Sermon on the Mount as he pens: "...heirs of the kingdom which He promised to those who love Him." Those who are spiritually bankrupt ("poor in spirit" cf. Matt. 5:3) shall inherit the kingdom of heaven. Is a man really poor if he is in the kingdom of heaven?

The term "kingdom of heaven" is an expression which is peculiar to Matthew's Gospel. It occurs 32 times. The word "kingdom" occurs 50 times. Yes, when the King comes from heaven to set up a kingdom on this earth, with heaven's standard (Matt. 5–7), the poor in spirit will be prominent as those rich in faith (Dan. 2:44; 7:14, 27). Praise God!

B. The COURTS Used for Oppression, 2:6. Verse 6 follows: "But you have dishonored the poor man." Throughout the Word of God, it is crystal clear that the Lord expects the believer to be merciful to the poor just as He is (cf. Job 5:15, 16; 36:15; Psa. 9:18; 68:10; 69:33; 72:12, 13;

102:17; 109:31; 113:7; 140:12; Jer. 20:13). As far as God is concerned, no one is a nonentity. All are important to Him. The world inevitably involves itself in preferential treatment on the bases of appearances. On the appearance of one's poor apparel, an individual is looked down upon as unimportant as if "the clothes make the man." Instead of receiving respect that he should as one with inherent dignity, he is discriminated against as one who really doesn't count or is not worth too much. As Zodiates says in plain down-to-earth language: "Don't steal his honor. He did not sacrifice it, as some have, for the sake of money, and for that he probably deserves more respect."

The poor were not only discriminated against in the places of worship but also were hauled into courts by the unsaved rich. The term "oppress" is a compound verb which means "to rule or have power." Therefore the word means to come down hard as in a potentate's rule; in other words, "to tyrannize." Poor Christians were being ruthlessly treated by the wealthy Jews (perhaps Sadducees, who were landowners). The words "drag you" is from an "old and vigorous word for violent treatment, as of Paul in Acts 16:19; 21:30" (Robertson). When the rich dragged the poor into court, they did so "personally!" This type of sick behavior also occurred in the Corinthian congregation (I Cor. 6:1-11).

Robertson summarizes:

> Rich Sadduccees had done this with Peter and John (Acts 4:1). As one of these potentates, yea, as a tyrant, Paul had once dragged men and women before the Sanhedrin (Acts 8:3; 22:4). He had even tried to make them blaspheme (Acts 26:11). It was not necessary to have special laws against the Christians. As objects of dislike it was easy enough, as Paul found out, to haul them into court. Paul came to know only too well how the tables could be turned on him when he became a Christian. He had to take his own medicine (Acts 13:50; 16:19). Jesus indeed had foretold that just this fate would befall his disciples before the courts of Jews and Gentiles (Matt. 10:17f.; John 16:2).

The word "court" in 2:6 is literally "courts" from the Greek word *criteria* from which we derive our English "criterion" which is a standard of judging. This word, according to Thayer, means "the instrument or means of trying or judging anything; the rule by which one judges" or "the place where judgment is given; the tribunal of a judge; a bench of judges."

It seems that many wealthy pagans are characteristically litigious. God help those who persecute the poor in the courts! They need to remember the words of Amos, who fearlessly heralded God's grave displeasure of the treatment of the downtrodden. Along this line, my friend Dr. Strauss gives a brief excerpt from a book by V. Raymond Edman, former President of Wheaton College:

> Someone had memory long enough to remember the gathering in Chicago in 1923 of the world's most successful financiers of that day and what became of them—
> Present were...
> The president of the largest independent steel company
> The greatest wheat speculator
> The president of the New York Stock Exchange
> A member of the President's Cabinet
> The greatest "bear" in Wall Street
> The president of the Bank of International Settlements
> The head of the world's greatest monopoly
>
> It has been well said that collectively these tycoons controlled more wealth than there was in the U. S. Treasury. Newspapers and magazines printed their success stories, urged American youth to follow their examples.
>
> Twenty-five years later, let's see what happened to these men...
>
> President of the largest steel company—Charles Schwab—lived on borrowed money the last five years of his life. He died "broke."
>
> Greatest wheat speculator—Arthur Cutten—dies abroad—insolvent.
>
> President of the New York Stock Exchange—Richard Whitney—was recently released from Sing Sing.
>
> The member of the President's Cabinet—Albert Fall—was pardoned from prison so he could die at home.
>
> The greatest "bear" in Wall Street—Jesse Livermore—committed suicide.
>
> President of the Bank of International Settlements—Leon Fraser—committed suicide.
>
> The head of the world's greatest monopoly—Ivar Krueger— committed suicide.
>
> Apparently winning is losing if material factors exceed the spiritual and moral, if selfish and sordid ends are pursued for self-promotion or pique, if increase is at the cost of integrity, and if intrigue be the price of preferment; while apparent losing is winning if there is the courage of convictions and adherence to principles of truth and justice.

The pattern of those who passionately practice a pecuniary-perspective and who persecute the poor is seen in:

C. The CLIMAX of James' Argument, 2:7. The climax of the argument against favoring the rich is that they "blaspheme the fair name by which you have been called." This is not the name "Christian" that is blasphemed, but the name of Jesus Christ Himself! Indeed, improper treatment of Christians is improper treatment of Christ. When Saul of Tarsus was persecuting the household of faith with an insurgent, barbarous onslaught, Christ intercepted him from heaven and said, "...I am Jesus whom you are persecuting" (Acts 9:5).

This is the same Lord Jesus Christ who for our sakes became poor (II Cor. 8:9). He was annointed to preach the Gospel to the poor (Luke 4:18). The poor were ever-present on His heart and therefore on His lips (Luke 14:13; 18:22; Matt. 19:21). The rich never impressed Him. They would give plenteous offerings to the synagogues, but Christ was unmoved by their copious contributions. It was no sacrifice for them, but the poor widow gave *ALL* (Luke 21:1-4). When the rich mistreat the poor, they are answerable to God! They blaspheme!

The word "blaspheme" means "to speak abusively, to rail, to calumniate, to often speak evil of men or things" (Used specifically of God: Rev. 16:11; the Holy Spirit: Luke 12:10; the divine name or doctrines: I Tim. 6:1).

When the wealthy come down on the poor with physical abuse, litigation or any oppressive treatment, they blaspheme the name of Christ. By means of this they speak evil of Him and His theocentric faith.

IV. THE PROPER PATTERN FOR PEOPLE, 2:8-9

A. The LAW, 2:8. It seems as if people of all eras have been status seekers. James speaks of all the status we will ever need in the term "the royal law." This is how one's activities may be governed. It is found in the Old Testament (Lev. 19:18; Deut. 6:5; 11:13). It is reiterated by the royal One Himself, King Jesus Christ (Matt. 22:35-40; Luke 10:15-37; John 13:34-35).

"Love" is that sovereign law, which has its source in heaven (I John 4:7). Love for God and man is fundamental to Christianity and therefore to life (Deut. 6:5). It is the greatest Biblical commandment and on it depends the whole law and the prophets (Matt. 22:40). Agape love is sacrificial concern and interest in the one loved.

This law is "according to the Scripture" which indicates that James adhered to the inspiration, inerrancy and infallibility of the Bible. James is stating that this law undergirds the teaching of impartiality. Love for one's neighbor is incompatible with partiality or prejudice. The "neighbor" is to be understood as "friend" (Thayer). A neighbor is not just anybody who has a need. James is not an advocate of the "social gospel." A friend is a brother in Christ who is in need. Therefore to practice the royal law of love is a mark that "you are doing well."

B. The LESSON, 2:9. "But if you show partiality, you are committing sin and are convicted by the law as transgressors." The word "if" should be rendered "since." The problem of "partiality" was being exhibited in this congregation. Therefore, "but," which is a strong word of contrast used to distinguish that the royal law of love was *not* being practiced "since you show partiality!" For this reason, "you are committing sin." Church sins are no less serious because they are committed in church. Partiality is not a *trifling fault*, it is a *foul travesty* of the law of God fully exposed in the Scriptures!

Because sin is sin, those who engage in partiality "are convicted by the law as transgressors." "Convicted" means that the proof of guilt was given. This proof was the Old Testament Mosaic law which condemned this very sin of partiality (Lev. 19:15; Deut. 1:17; 16:19). These were Christian, Jewish "transgressors."

V. THE POINT OF THE PRECEPTS, 2:10-11

Without a doubt, verse 9 was a hard saying. The law convicts those who persist in partiality and prejudice as transgressors. How is God's law transgressed by those who cater to the rich and neglect the poor?

Because, my dear friend, sin is sin. There are no categories of sin as to their seriousness. Let me explain.

In my first book, *God Has a Better Idea*, I listed some contrasts in Matthew 5:21-47. There Christ was setting forth the principles of righteousness in contrast to the Pharisees. To the legalist, the big sin was murder; but, it was no big thing to hate in his heart. Christ said there was *no* difference.

I have seen "model" church members, board members, deacons and deaconesses appear to be ideal Christians. But, these very same people have practiced partiality, maligned men and women with vicious tongue and have been down right dispiteous, despicable and evil. When they are confronted, they deny it and sometimes are not even aware of the damage they are causing.

These saints do not commit murder or steal or any other "biggies." But, they verbally assault, hate in their heart, cause divisions in churches, drive away new people from the congregation and a host of other "little" sins.

As Dr. Robertson adds:

...those who were guilty of spiritual pride and other sins boasted of their freedom from adultery and murder (Hort)...murder springs out of hate and that all of God's laws come from the same will (Mayor). It is disobedience to the will of God that constitutes the essence of sin. It is not a light matter to be guilty of any sin.

The poor, completed Jew, who had embraced the messiahship of Jesus, had probably been all too familiar with the pseudo-religiosity and hypocrisy of the traditionalist leadership. Needless to say, some baby Christians were greatly influenced by their religious leaders. Some of their rabbinical authorities differentiated between large and small sins and "regarded certain laws like the Sabbath regulations as more crucially necessary...Shemoth Rabb, XXV says, 'This Sabbath weighs against all the precepts: if they kept it, they were reckoned as having done all'" (Rosscup). In addition, the Rabbis considered Christianity as a cult and sometimes viewed it merely as an adjunct of Judaism rather than the full-blown messianic hope. Therefore they would make life miserable for the Christian Jew and excuse their brutal behavior toward them as merely doing God a favor.

Brothers and sisters, don't allow your Christianity to be "Churchianity." There are no large and small sins. The point of the precepts is if one violates one part of the law, he violates all of it! Therefore using James' illustration, if one abstains from adultery, but murders another man, he cannot congratulate himself for observing one part of the law and ignoring the dastardly deed of homicide.

You see, these Jewish leaders would emphasize or de-emphasize portions of the law for their own expedient activities. Believe it or not the idea of sexual sin was really no big issue at this time of Israeli history. All of the historians agree that the Sanhedrin never enforced the laws against adultery because of the notoriously frequent cases. Also, many of these hypocrite leaders of religion were so entrenched in adultery themselves that they didn't dare bring it to public light. But murder and adultery and gossip are all equally as bad for all three are SIN! But the Rabbis had "The Big Three Sins": murder, idolatry and adultery. In fact Leviticus postulates: "...the adulterer and the adulteress shall surely be put to death" (20:10).

True, God views adultery as a very serious sin because it destroys the basic unit of society—the family. The Mishna (a set of codified laws) said that the penalty for adultery was to be execution by strangulation. Of course, the Mishna came after the Mosaic Law and altered it somewhat. At any rate, this is a paraphrased quotation from the Mishna: "The man is to be enclosed in dung up to his knees. Then a soft towel, wrapped in a rough towel, is to be tightened around his neck. Two men pull in either direction until he is dead."

The Jewish members of James' Christian congregation were most enlightened about the Pharaisaic methods of emphasizing some sins and deemphasizing others as they themselves would participate in them. James says that the sin of partiality is as bad as the actions of the Pharisees. All who sin, whether glossing over it or not, are lawbreakers! That is a stark reality, a blunt fact and the music must be faced!

VI. THE PROSPECT OF PERFECTION, 2:12-13

A. The DEMEANOR of the Law of Liberty, 2:12. There will be "Pay Day Some Day" for all human beings. The writer to the Hebrews enjoins: "...it is appointed for men to die once, and after this comes judgment" (Heb. 9:27). There are two future judgments: (1) The Bema Seat of Christ where the words of believers will be evaluated (II Cor. 5:10; Matt. 12:36; Rom. 14:10; Gal. 6:7; Eph. 6:8; Col. 3:24-25). This is not a judgment for sin since the Christian's sins have been atoned for and are remembered no more forever (Heb. 10:17). Then there is (2) The Great White Throne Judgment where will be gathered all who have rejected the provision of Christ from the beginning of human history (Rev. 20:11-15). The evaluation of believers' works is what James refers to in verse 12.

"So speak and so act" is in the present tense and indicates that this should be the habit pattern and the mood of command is used to instruct these believers that proper demeanor is mandatory. It is obligatory because they are "as those who are to be judged by the law of liberty."

"...by the law of liberty" goes back to 1:25. The word "liberty" is used 11 times in the New Testament. James uses it (1:25 and 2:12) to remind his Jewish audience that they are not meticulously bound as a Pharisaical legalist nor a Judaizer, who must rigidly observe a collection of codified regulations. The spirit is of immensely more magnitude than the letter (II Cor. 3:6). We are under grace, not law!

B. The DESTINY of the Merciless, 2:13. But verse 13 is a heavy duty warning: "For judgment will be merciless to one who has shown no mercy; mercy triumphs over judgment." Charles R. Erdman reinforces: "We should be careful, then, as to our judgments, and guard against all unfair discriminations, all narrow suspicions and class distinctions and race prejudices, for we ourselves are to be judged." Those professing believers who showed no mercy upon others in need, will be given no mercy. The one who displays mercy toward needy men and women, as a habit of life, reveals that he is a Christian (Matt. 5:7; 6:14-15; 18:35; Ps. 18:25-26).

But the individual who does not disseminate mercy toward others, as a pattern of his overall life, will ultimately be the recipient of God's judgment.

However, praise be to God: "mercy triumphs over judgment." The scholarly Dr. Rosscup clearly and accurately summarizes:

> When a man lives without mercy to others in God's world, he simply shows off the fact that he himself has never responded aright to the immeasurable mercy of God....The mercy a man has shown others as fruit of a life touched by God's saving mercy will triumph over judgment. His own sins, worthy of judgment, are removed by God's working in his life dissolves all the charges strict justice might bring against him. Thus his showing of mercy is not a matter of heaping up personal merit to deserve salvation by his own good works. The mercy he shows is itself a work of God for which he can take no credit.

The Colors
of the
Household of Faith

THE CHAPTER OUTLINED:

The purpose of this presentation is to cause the Christian to do more than just sit around and contemplate. Christianity is "where the action is." This action demonstrates faith. Yes, we are *saved* to *serve*; however, we don't *serve* to become *saved*! Indeed, the teacher must challenge his students to "expect great things *from* God and attempt great things *for* God!"

The discussion on faith and works in the second chapter, verses 14-26 is a hotly contested passage among theologians. It was this section of James which caused the renowned Martin Luther to title this book as an "epistle of straw."

Luther thought that James should not even be a part of the canon since it contradicted the epistles of Paul. Luther, as a former Augustinian monk was "programmed" into earning his way to heaven by means of indulgences, penances and good works. He fasted for weeks, tortured himself for his sins in very hideous and grotesque ways to merit the "Divine Favor" and appease a very angry God. Then, one day, in the privacy of his deep and thorough study of the Pauline Epistles of Romans and Galatians, he almost had a tramautic seizure when he discovered that the teachings of Scripture and the dogmas of the Roman Catholic Church absolutely did not jibe.

Martin Luther, as he was led by the Holy Spirit, was enlightened to the fundamental truth that salvation is not the result of any human activity, but *only* through faith in the finished work of Jesus Christ Himself. Even Habakkuk said, "…but the righteous will live by his faith" (Hab. 2:4; cf. Rom. 1:17; Gal. 3:11). It was this monumental truth, which leaped from the pages before him that consummated the salvation of Martin Luther.

"When," said Luther, "by the Spirit of God I understood these words, 'the righteous will live by his faith,' I felt born again like a new man; I entered through the open doors into the very paradise of God!"

Obviously, Luther's background and Roman Catholic indoctrination greatly garnished his perspective toward James. But, in reality there is *no* conflict between the writings of either Paul or James as I hope to demonstrate in this chapter.

I. THE PROBLEM OF PIOUS PRETENSE, 2:14-17

Since James is devastatingly down to earth about faith, and will tolerate no shams, he underscores a problem which he will not allow any of his readers to shirk. He presents two questions in verse 14, both of which demand a resounding affirmative. These two questions prove that:

A. Pious Pretense Cannot SAVE, 2:14. To demonstrate that pious pretense cannot save, James asks in question one:

1. **"What use is it,** my brethren, if a man says he has faith, but he has no works?" The words "if a man says" is a third class condition in the Greek (just as in 2:15, 17). In other words, maybe a man will say this, and maybe he will not, but for the sake of argument, let us assume that he does make such a claim and yet has not works. "Say" is in the present tense and reveals that this man is continually professing faith. But James maintains that it is not *saying* but *showing* which proves that one is saved. The second question of 2:14 is:

2. **"Can that faith save him?"** James relentlessly presses on with the uncomfortable question. In essence, he says put your life where your mouth is. John speaks of this in his first epistle (I John 1:6): "If we say that we have fellowship with Him and yet walk in the darkness, we lie and do not practice the truth." Here is a man who claims to be a Christian (that is, professor); this was probably a reference to a man of the heretical Gnostic error in the Early Church. But, his habit or pattern of life contradicted his claim. He was a walking contradiction. Therefore his profession was a "lie" from the Greek word which stressed false character. This one is living a lie!

Back in James 2:14, the phrase "that faith" is literally "the faith." In the context, it refers to the first question in verse 14 which concerned a man's professional faith without works. The question anticipates a negative answer (Robertson). In other words, "no, *that* faith is not able to save him." Pseudo faith is not able to save! "Only genuine faith is saving faith. Any other type of faith is actually not faith at all" (Rosscup). Not only does pious pretense not save; but,

B. Pious Pretense Doesn't SERVE, 2:15-17. James says to "get off the dime" and demonstrate that your faith is genuine. He sets up a "for real" situation to illustrate his point. The "if" of verse 15 is our familiar third class condition. Therefore, let us assume that a brother or sister in Christ "is without clothing and in need of daily food." There is not sufficient provision for even daily sustenance (cf. Matt. 3:4; 10:10; 24:45; Heb. 5:12-14; Matt. 25:36ff). These needy ones are members of the congregation and another from among the assembly merely "says" some pious platitudes which amount to nothing! For example: "I'll pray for you, but I can't get involved personally!" It takes warm clothes and warm food to keep one satisfied, not just warm words. It takes a *work not a word* to fill an empty stomach. True faith works by love (Gal. 5:6). Believers are to "do good to all men, and especially to those of the household of the faith" (Gal. 6:10). Needy Christians need more than nice sounding words, they need someone who is moved to help them and does!

Dr. Strauss writes:

> If a man does not show love toward those in need, he thereby shows that his faith is not a true and living one. Lip service to the principle of Christianity is no proof that one is saved. You may go so far as to pray for those in need, but without corresponding action, your prayers and testimonies constitute hypocrisy in its worst form. What profit is your profession of faith to you, or to anyone else, if you dismiss the needy with prayers and good wishes while you withhold from them the necessities of life?

When the needs of people are apparent and you say, "'Go in peace, be warmed and be filled'; and yet do not give them what is necessary for their body, what use is that?" (2:16). The Apostle John adds his comment to this statement of James': "But whoever has the world's goods, and beholds his brother in need and closes his heart against him, how does the love of God abide in him? Little children, let us not love with word or with tongue, but in deed and truth" (I John 3:17-18). If a man says (a professor) that God's love is in him, he will be concerned about the welfare of those who know the Lord. Love which is only talk is not love at all. Prove your love by your good works. The manner of life will be characterized by self-sacrificial sharing with brothers and sisters who are in need. Donald W. Burdick writes: "...love is not to be merely a matter of speech, merely the meaningless exercises of the tongue...love is to be a matter of action."

Verse 17 is the clincher. It illustrates what is wrong with professed faith which fails to follow the law of love. It says, "Even so faith, if it has not works, is dead, being by itself." When something is dead, the animation principle is departed. Corpses do not make public appearances, neither do they sing or play. Self-professed faith is dead because it does not work! Faith minus works is "dead!"

II. THE PANACEA FOR PIOUS PRETENSE, 2:18-20

This is seen in:

A. A Dynamic DEMONSTRATION, 2:18. Once again the extreme practicality of James is revealed. The statement of verse 18 smashes the phoney facade of empty profession. James supposes a very real challenge a man might make to put faith to the "acid test."

"But someone may well say" introduces a pleasant change of pace.

Here, for a refreshing change, is a man's *saying* something that is on the side of *possessing* faith and not *professing* faith as in verses 14 and 16. This man has got it all together in his life for the Lord. The challenge is made by this man, "You have faith and I have works; show me your faith without the works, and I will show you my faith by my works" (James 2:18). The lines are drawn which separate the men from the boys in the area of faith. Notice the distinction: **The Professor**—"You have faith" (glibly professed)...**The Possessor**—"I have deeds." **The Professor**—"Show me your faith without the deeds"...**The Possessor**— "I will show you my faith by my deeds."

Faith without deeds is unproductive, dead and unprofitable. But, genuine saving faith is productive and it is alive! Where there is life, there is activity. Where there is faith there is works or actions. This is faith in "overalls"—it is working faith!

Well, only works demonstrate that we have faith. "So then, you will know them by their fruits" (Matt. 7:20). Jesus knows what is in man (John 2:24-25). Just because one believes that God can do miracles means nothing. One must *believe in* God. Genuine faith must precede works to make them good (Matt. 7:21-23). Faith produces works (John 6:28-29; I John 3:23; Eph. 3:8-10; Titus 2:11-14; 3:8). "Good" works are *only* for Christians for they are dynamic demonstrations of faith. Therefore the Christian should be eager to get into the game. Standing on the sidelines is never as much fun as playing in the game.

B. Demonic DELUSIONS, 2:19. James selects another case to illustrate his proposition (2:14) that faith without works is dead and unable to save (2:17), but that faith with works is effectual to save (2:18). Indeed, belief without works is dead; in fact, the one who professes to be a Christian and is not productive is suffering from an acute case of demonic delusion.

The nouns, Satan and demons, are in and of themselves frightening. Satan's desire is to so captivate one's mind in the bondage of fear that one expects the devil to leap from under his bed at night. Even Satan's cabals have a fearsome aura of mystery about them. Satan and all his cohorts "shudder" with a realization that God is going to "lower the boom" on them forever (Matt. 8:29; Mark 1:24). All of their little capers here on planet earth will come to a screeching halt for they will scream in hell forever (Rev. 19:20—20:3, 10; 22:15).

As James writes these words concerning the demons literally "bristling up" with fear in conviction of their impending doom, his first century readers are Jewish and this statement is of special significance to them.

You see, the Jew maintained an orthodox belief in one God (monotheism) and in that sense his doctrine was straight (Deut. 6:4; Mark 12:29; Eph. 4:6). The Hebrews are to be commended for this in that their teaching did not conform to the pagans, which were all around them, who espoused belief in many gods (polytheism). As far as this was concerned, James says, "You do well." They give total mental assent to the existence of the one, true God (namely, Jehovah). But, "the demons also believe" and "shudder." Robertson says concerning this word "shudder" that it is an "old onomato-poetic verb to bristle up, to shudder, only here in the New Testament. It is like the Latin *horreo* (horror, standing of the hair on end with terror). The demons do more than believe a fact. They shudder at it."

James postulates to his Hebrew brothers that they are to make sure that there is no smug complacency in their belief. It must be more than a "head" knowledge. It must be a "heart" knowledge if it is to be vital. There has to be a personal relationship with the one, true God, not just an acknowledgment of the fundamental facts about His oneness. Even the demons retain that! Yes, not only will atheists be in hell; but, the Bible tells us that hell will be loaded with people who believe in God! There is more to faith than just believing the facts. One must personally appropriate. The key phrase, "if a man says," refers to mere lip service; empty profession; but, no possession of life inside. A man may know everything about the Bible and about God; but, if there is no personal relationship with Christ, there is no salvation. It is simply:

C. A Dead DISPLAY, 2:20. James blasts away, "But are you willing to recognize, you foolish fellow, that faith without works is useless?" If a man's profession does not go any farther than the belief of the demons, then that man is a "foolish fellow." The Greek word *kene* means "empty" (I Cor. 15:36). The linguistic scholar R. C. Trench comments, "When used not of things but of persons *kenos* predicates not merely an absence and emptiness of good, but, since the moral nature of man endures no vacuum, the presence of the contrary."

As we look deeper into verse 20 we learn some crucial truths. "Faith" means "to persuade." In the King James Version the noun is rendered "assurance" once, "belief" once, "faith" 239 times, "fidelity" once, "them that believe" once, and "he which believeth" once. It basically means "faith, belief, trust and confidence" (Abbott-Smith).

The words "without deeds" is the apparent cause of the friction that Martin Luther had with the Book of James. "Deeds" is from the Greek *ergon* from which we derive our English "energy" and means "work, task and employment" (Abbott-Smith). The term ergophobia means a "fear of work" which was a malady I contracted in college. God has arrested ergophobia in me through a love of His Word (II Tim. 2:15). (Ergon *does not produce salvation, but s*alvation produces *ergon.* The *Wycliffe Bible Commentary* says:

> Most of the difficulties in the interpretation of 2:14-26 have arisen out of a failure to understand that: (1) James was not refuting the Pauline doctrine of justification by faith but rather a perversion of it; (2) Paul and James used the words *works* and *justification* in different senses.

Weiss's commentary purports:

> James says faith without being proved by works is useless. He is not contending against dogmatic doctrines, but he is exposing the self-deception which is found in this, that we content ourselves with mere faith. ...Just as the charity, which finds its expression only in empty words, is of no use, if at the same time it does not bring help in need; thus, too, faith is worthless if it does not at the same time prove itself to be living by working what it should work.

Faith is useless if it doesn't accomplish the intended purpose of bringing service to others. The truth of the matter is seen in:

III. THE PROOF OF PRODUCTIVITY, 2:21-26

Producing fruit is proof positive that one's faith is real. Is this any way to live your life? What could be greater than to serve Him and glorify Him? (I Cor. 10:31). And James uses three more illustrations to show that real faith will eventually prove, through deeds, that it is genuine. Again, it is necessary to reiterate that this epistle does not teach that a man is saved through works; but, on down-the-road of life, in God's eternal game plan, faith by deeds will be shown to be the real thing! The three illustrations are: (1) The Case of Abraham, 2:21-24; (2) The Case of Rahab, 2:25; (3) The Case of the Body without the Spirit, 2:26. First, let us consider:

A. The Case of ABRAHAM, 2:21-23. In the estimation of any Jew, two of the highest ranking, Hebrew heroes are Moses and Abraham. During my last visit to Israel, I toured an olive wood factory. It was there that I purchased some most beautiful olive wood statues of Moses for my family and certain close friends. He is highly regarded (John 8:33,39).

Mothers in the United States name their children Mike, Steve or Dave; but, in Israel, a most common name is Moses. Most everyone has heard of Moshe Dayan, the great Israeli general, who was the hero of the Six Day War. Moshe Dayan in Hebrew means "Moses is judge."

In keeping with the interest of his Jewish audience, it is logical that James would cite Abraham as an illustration of his point. That is: a man is justified in the sense that he has true *faith* that works (2:23). Abraham is an apt example of faith and its result. His name appears in the New Testament 74 times, most of these in particular reference to his faith (cf. Acts 7; Rom. 4; Gal. 3; Heb. 11). Dr. Rosscup elucidates, "Every Jew (and Gentile Christian) looks to him as 'father' of faith, and so James can expose the reality or the pretense of a man's profession of faith by asking him to examine genuinely faith in action." Let us study the following three things about the justification of Abraham:

1. The Method of His Justification, (2:21). The method of Abraham's justification was "by works." But works never saved anyone (Eph. 2:8-9). Therefore, Abraham, just like you and me, is saved by faith (Gen. 15:6 and Rom. 4:1-5). He was "justified" or declared righteous! His faith was justified before men being already saved since the Genesis 22:15-18 event took place at least 30 years after the time of Genesis 15:6.

In Genesis 15:6 we read, "Then he *believed* in the Lord; and He reckoned it to him as righteousness." In other words, Abraham was justified by his belief, his faith! When Abraham was willing to offer Isaac in Genesis 22:15-18, particularly 22:16, he demonstrated his faith in a work of obedience. His faith was completed by his works in the eyes of man. You see, a man can only see faith as it *blossoms* into *works*. God can see the *bud*.

James is not contradicting Paul! James' phrase "justified by works" does not contradict Romans 4:1-5, where Paul writes that it was the faith of Abraham that was his method of justification and salvation. (Rom. 4:9). "But Paul is talking about the faith of Abraham before his circumcision (4:10) as the basis of his being set right with God, which faith is symbolized in the circumcision. James makes plain his meaning also" (Robertson). James says, "...when he offered up Isaac his son on the altar." James and Paul use the same words, but speak of different acts. Robertson continues:

> James points to the offering of Isaac on the altar (Gen. 22:16ff) as *proof* of the faith that Abraham already had. Paul discusses Abraham's faith as the basis of his justification, that and not his circumcision. There is no contradiction at all between James and Paul.

Permit me to use this equation to show that *both* James and Paul are saying: Profession of faith ⟶ production of works + salvation.

2. The Meaning of His Justification, 2:22. James further elaborates with his readers as he logically reasons out his premise. Being Jews, very legalistically and works-oriented, I am certain they had their "Moment of Aha." This is when the light comes on in your head and you grasp the meaning of something and say, "Aha! That is what that means!" So he presses home his meaning in verse 22.

"You see?" he asks. "That faith was working with his works." The word *sunergei* translated "working with" in the text means "was cooperating, was helping." In other words, faith and works go hand in hand. The works were the accompaniment, the completion, the expression of faith. As the Greeks would say, *"Eureka!"* Abraham was declared righteous by faith; however, the faith worked because it was true faith.

"As a result of the works," James pens, "faith was perfected." "Perfected" means that Abraham's faith was brought to the end of a process; it was completed. The passive mood shows that God was the One who brought his faith to its goal.

3. The Motive of His Justification, 1:23. The motive of father Abraham's justification was that "the Scripture was fulfilled." Dr. Robertson establishes:

> So James quotes Genesis 15:6 as proving his point in verse 21 that Abraham had works with his faith, the very same passage that Paul quotes in Romans 4:3 to show that Abraham's faith preceded his circumcision and was the basis of his justification.

Then he believed in the Lord; and He reckoned it to him as righteousness" (Gen. 15:6). The word "reckoned" is a business term and was used in accounting (Rom. 6:11,13). It was "logged" to Abraham's account.

Verse 23 goes on to state, "and he was called the friend of God." In my humble opinion, this is the greatest compliment that could ever be given, — "friend of God." James' Jewish audience would certainly be familiar with two Old Testament Scriptures where the old patriarch is so designated (II Chron. 20:7 and Isa. 41:8). In the Isaiah passage, Jehovah refers to the aged Abraham as "My friend." Did not Jesus make the same connection between faith and works when He said, "You are My friends, if you do what I command you" (John 15:14).

4. The Man Justified, 2:24. Verse 24 is actually the conclusive reply to the questions of verse 14. "Bare, unproductive faith, cannot save a man. True faith will demonstrate itself in works, and only such a faith brings justification" (Wessel). The faith that justifies is faith that results in assiduous labor and thorough procedure of living. Works do not save a man. The man who is justified is a man whose faith produces arduous works! Rosscup again aids us in contrasting James' words, "by faith only," with Paul's in order to realize the complete harmony between them:

Paul (Romans 4)	James
Faith alone brings justification. But this is faith of living reality that works, for Paul begins and closes his epistle to the Romans with a clear emphasis upon the *obedience* of the type of faith he is writing about (1:5; 16:19).	Faith alone does not justify (v. 24). James has in view the spurious type of so-called faith which some professed but did not work. Actually it was not faith at all. By this pseudo faith, a man cannot be justified. But James would agree with Paul that a man can be justified by genuine faith which expresses its living quality in works.

B. The Case of RAHAB, 2:25. "Rahab the harlot" is under consideration. In the eyes of Jewry, it is probably no big thing to argue for Abraham's justification. So, to cover the entire gamut of life's experiences, James goes from a *saint* to a *streetwalker*. Rahab was a prostitute, a woman and a Gentile; none of which was too highly regarded by Hebrews. The logic is: if she can be saved, anyone can be saved.

The story of Rahab is recorded in Joshua chapters 2 and 6. The evidence of her faith is expressed: "I know that the Lord has given you the land...for the Lord your God, He is God in heaven above and on earth beneath" (Joshua 2:9, 11). All the city of Jericho had the opportunity to repent as did Rahab. She recognized the Lord and did so. It is never right to do wrong to do right! But, Rahab in her infant faith thought that the end justified the means and she lied to protect the Israeli spies. God did not bless her lie; but, in her lie was faith that identified her with God and His people, and before men she was justified. This is a real commitment and it occurred under extremely adverse circumstances. The writer in Hebrews says, "By faith Rahab the harlot did not perish along with those who were disobedient, after she had welcomed the spies in peace" (Heb. 11:31). It needs to be said that Rahab became a changed woman and forsook the world's oldest occupation, prostitution. As a matter of fact, the Jewish Midrash states that Rahab married General Joshua and became an ancestor of Jeremiah and Ezekiel.

C. The Case of a BODY WITHOUT THE SPIRIT, 2:26. Here is another clear-cut analogy. A man is a "body," which is his material part and he is a "spirit," which is his immaterial part. If there is life, it is not an either/or situation, but a both/and. If the immaterial portion is separated from the material, then death results. A man is justified when he has *faith* (this would be the true spiritual essence or substance of his life) and *works* that are inseparably related to it and the manifestation (expression of its living reality). The two come together. Living faith involves works just as much as a living spirit has a body.

Dear friend, you and I have it all! We have climbed the mountain through faith! Our good deeds are proof that we produce because we live by faith. All Christians should always be busy in good works for Christ. Indolence is incompatible with Christ. The maxim is true: "If you want something done, ask a busy person to do it!" Moses was with his flocks at Horeb. Gideon was threshing wheat by the wine press. David was caring for his father's sheep. Elisha was plowing with twelve yolk of oxen. Nehemiah was bearing the king's cup. Amos was following the flock. Peter and Andrew were casting a net into the sea. James and John were mending their nets. Matthew was collecting customs. Saul was persecuting Christians. William Carey was mending shoes.

Your church is looking for people who are busy—not busy earning salvation—but busy serving the Lord for He has already given to them His salvation. Your Lord and your church are looking for people who will step forward and let it be known that they want to be busy doing God's business.

A Maze
of Mouth

THE CHAPTER OUTLINED:

The evils of the tongue must be seen. Whenever a person says, "Did you hear what…" or "Did you hear the latest about…" or "Did you know that…"—BEWARE! Gossip is about to gush forth! Some believers try to garnish their gossip with "Christian concern" which still spreads the latest naughty news so that you might "pray." (Isn't that pious?) Next to the ignorance of the Scriptures, the greatest danger to our churches is the tongue!

I. MASTERS MUST TAME THE TONGUE, 3:1

The King James Version (1611) says: "My brethren, be not many masters…." The New American Standard Bible renders the same phrase: "Let not many of you become teachers, my brethren…." "Masters" was a 1611 term used to describe our twentieth century word "teachers."

The reader might be wondering why there appears to be an abrupt change in thought between chapters 2 and 3. Actually, there is no change at all; only a reiteration of the same thing. In chapter 2, James has been writing about the "professor," the one who *says* (2:14, 16, 18). Yet, there is no concrete work to prove his claims. He has no deeds to backup his statements. So, James takes the subject of speech a step further. Empty statements that merely claim can degenerate into abusive and destructive talk. For sure, this does not reflect the evidence of genuine conversion any way (3:13, 17).

I believe that James begins at the proper place in 3:1—"right at the pinacle of the Jewish religious strata-teachers, prominent for using their tongues. Thus he shows that hypocrisy is a peril for all men from the top down" (Rosscup).

Remember that James is writing to the Christian Jews of the *Diaspora*. Therefore, he is thoroughgoing with examples from Jewish life to illustrate his points. Here is another one. It was considered most prestigious for a family to have a son who was training for the rabbinate. The rabbinical training was status in the ancient world. Therefore, young men would compete with one another for the privilege of being admitted to "Rabbi School." The honors and powers of a Rabbi were most motivating forces.

When Christianity began to convert many in the first century synagogues, the competition compounded. Who could be the best teachers became status symbol number two. So "silver-tongued" oratory was the means of achieving the limelight in the synagogues. Rather than preach, pray and plug away for God's glory, they were exercising their tongues for the approval of man.

Realizing this potent problem, James exhorts: "Let not many of you become teachers...." He was desirous of restricting the number of teachers in the Christian movement. Why? Because greater knowledge means greater responsibility (Matt. 18:6; Luke 12:48; James 4:17).

Today, there is a dearth of preachers. I guess I can see why. The pay is atrocious. The benefits are worse. And the hours are double *any* union maximum! No wonder the Lord offers a special reward just for the pastor-teacher (I Peter 5:1-4). But, the truth of James is still applicable today. Those who aspire to the office of a pastor-teacher should do so "knowing that as such we shall incur a stricter judgment." Paul's words are true: "...if a man aspires to the office of an overseer, it is a fine work he desires to do" (I Tim. 3:1). But there must be long and deep soul-searching and prayer before preparing for the pastorate. There is serious accountability before the Lord. Sometimes the parishioner forgets the seriousness of the office of his pastor and becomes critical of him. For example, the Rev. Henry Ward Beecher entered Plymouth Church one Sunday and found several letters awaiting him. He opened one and found it contained the single word, "Fool." Quietly and with becoming seriousness he announced to the congregation the fact in these words: "I have known many an instance of a man writing a letter and forgetting to sign his name, but this is the only instance I have ever known of a man signing his name and forgetting to write the letter."

The word "teacher" *(didaskaloi)*, in its noun form is found only in Acts 13:1, I Corinthians 12:18, Ephesians 4:11 and here (James 3:1). The pastor's primary responsibility is to be a teacher. He is to study more than he does anything else. As a matter of fact, the pastor is worth twice as much to his people financially if he "works hard at preaching and teaching" (I Tim. 5:17-18). This stands to reason since he will "incur a stricter judgment."

The teachers of the congregation are to use their tongues to edify the people (Acts 20:32). This is because they assume a great responsibility before the Lord. Dear churchman, don't be critical of your pastor because he doesn't do what you think he is to do. His "job description" is in the Bible. If you don't follow him, you are in deep trouble. Consider Hebrews 13:17: "Obey your leaders, and submit to them; for they keep watch over your souls, as those who will give an account. Let them do this with joy and not with grief, for this would be unprofitable for you."

II. MATURITY AND THE TAMING OF THE TONGUE, 3:2

The content and character of one's conversation is an indicator of his maturity. People who gossip simply are immature (spiritually, and perhaps mentally, as well). These are those who major in minors.

James writes in 3:2, "For we all stumble in many ways." Even the teachers, who are seemingly mature in Christ, often stumble. A teacher may stumble "in what he says" probably more than any other area. Dr. Robertson remarks, "The teacher uses his tongue constantly and so is in particular peril on this score." Zodiates adds:

> The more we say, the more we are likely to stumble. The more we do for Christ, the more mistakes we are likely to make and the more criticisms we are likely to incur. The most criticized person in the house of God is the most active one in both words and deeds. The person who does nothing is seldom criticized.

In James 3:2, "the perfect man" is the mature man. The more successfully one controls his tongue, the more mature he is. The man who can tame his tongue is a man who is "able to bridle the whole body as well." In other words, if a man can control the emissions from his mouth, he can control his entire body. Dr. Robertson summarizes, "James apparently means that the man who bridles his tongue does not stumble in speech and is able also to control his whole body with all its passions. See Titus 1:11 about stopping people's mouths."

The term "bridle" is dealt with more extensively in verse 3. This is seen in:

III. MODELS FOR TAMING THE TONGUE, 3:3-8

The tongue is the most difficult member to control in spite of its size. It is mentioned directly or indirectly in every chapter of the Epistle of James (1:19, 26; 2:12; chap. 3; 4:11; 5:12). The tongue, as a deadly destructive device, is pictured throughout God's Book.

For example, the physician says, "Ah"; but, Paul says, "Their throat is an open grave, with their tongues they keep deceiving, the poison of asps is under their lips; whose mouth is full of cursing and bitterness" (Rom. 3:13-14). Job comments, "...I lay my hand on my mouth" (Job 40:4). Moses is recorded as having committed some outlandish sins, including murder. But the sin for which he received the most dire punishment was the sin of his lips. "They also provoked Him to wrath at the waters of Meribah, so that it went hard with Moses on their account; because they were rebellious against His Spirit, he spoke rashly with his lips (Ps. 106:32-33).

Brethren, Jesus Christ Himself, the epitome of our example, controlled His speech. "...Christ also suffered for you, leaving you an example for you to follow in His steps, who committed no sin, nor was any deceit found in His mouth" (I Peter 2:21-22). Isaiah shares what is pertinent: "...Woe is me, for I am ruined! Because I am a man of unclean lips, and I live among a people of unclean lips; for my eyes have seen the King, the Lord of hosts. Then one of the seraphim flew to me, with a burning coal in his hand which he had taken from the altar with tongs. And he touched my mouth with it and said, 'Behold, this has touched your lips; and your iniquity is taken away and your sin is forgiven' " (Isa. 6:5-7). Therefore, it is readily apparent that the tongue is *the* final battleground and the final member to be placed on the altar. Give it to God!

James goes on to present four models to illustrate how one's control over a small thing gives him control over a large thing. Control a horse's mouth and one can control the direction of his entire body; control the helm of a sailing vessel and one controls the movements of the entire ship; control a small fire in the forest, and one keeps it from destroying the whole forest; the trainer can control his animal.

A. The Horse and the Bit, 3:3. "Now if we put" could be rendered "since." "The bits into the horses' mouths" sets up the illustration. The purpose is "so that they may obey us." The result is that the riders "direct their entire body as well."

A. B. Simpson, founder of the Christian and Missionary Alliance, summarizes verse 3:

> Just as a man's mouth is the test of his character, so the horse's mouth is the place to control him. We put bits in their mouths, and by these turn about their whole body, so that a little bit of steel and a little thong of leather will hold a fiery steed, and turn him at the touch of a woman's hand. So the tongue is like a bridle, which can be put upon us. With a fiery horse you put a curb in his bit. The idea is to hurt him, if he pulls against the bit. So God has given to us checks upon our tongue, making it hurt us, if we speak unadvisedly.

God's Word is true. "The grass withers, the flower fades, but the word of our God stands forever" (Isa. 40:8). These sayings about the tongue will stand forever. "Do not be as the horse or as the mule which have no understanding: whose trappings include bit and bridle to hold them in check..." (Ps. 32:9). The Scriptures tell us that Samson "found a new jawbone of an ass, and put it forth in his hand, and took it, and slew a thousand men with it" (Judges 15:15—The New Scofield Reference Bible). Ironically enough, there are those who slay each day the same number of people with the same weapon!

B. The Rudder and the Ship, 3:4. This nautical metaphor draws imagery to point out the tremendous effect and power of the tongue. It is compared to the small rudder that directs the ship. These little rudders are able to manipulate those huge ships even when they are driven "by strong winds." And, this control is "wherever the inclination of the pilot desires." If the steersman makes a mistake he can sink the ship. Brother, sister, what you can do with your tongue is immense.

Dr. Sweeting, president of the Moody Bible Institute, comments:

> One slogan used during World War II was "a slip of the lip may sink a ship." I have a picture of a South Pacific battle scene in which marines are storming a beachhead. They are dropping everywhere. One marine is wounded and bleeding. The picture bears a two-word title: "Somebody Talked." It may be that the tongue has slain more than have all the bullets and bombs of battle.

The Book of Proverbs exhorts, "...And a soft tongue breaks the bone" (25:15). Again, Proverbs: "The one who guards his mouth preserves his life; the one who opens wide his lips comes to ruin" (13:3).

"What the rudder is to the ship, the tongue is to the body. James is saying that to avoid shipwreck—control your tongue!" (Sweeting).

C. Fire and the Forest, 3:5-6. The prolific pen of James continues with another vivid portrayal of the perils of the tongue. Perhaps if James knew that someday there would be such a thing as a smog device, he probably would have issued them for the mouths of some of his readers.

"So also the tongue is a small part of the body." Just like the bridle and the rudder are small in comparison to a horse and ship, so the tongue is small compared to the body. "And yet it [the tongue] boasts of great things." In other words, it is a small part, but talks big.

Here in sunny Southern California, forest fires break out every summer. Most of these titanic infernos are triggered by matches or cigarettes tossed from an automobile by a smoking motorist. A friend of mine is a captain in the Los Angeles Fire Department. He says that the heat from one of these blazes is so intense that there have been cases where the protective clothing has literally melted and became meshed with the men's skin. Huge, hellish holocausts result from one small cigarette. This is James' thought, "Behold, how great a forest is set aflame by such a small fire!" Just as in Southern California (which is similar to Mediterranean climate), in the ancient world forest fires were most frequent. This was true especially in Lebanon with the multitudinous cedars.

Morgan Blake, sportswriter for the *Atlanta Journal*, wrote:

> I am more deadly than the screaming shell from the howitzer. I

win without killing. I tear down homes, break hearts, and wreck lives. I travel on the wings of the wind. No innocence is strong enough to intimidate me, no purity pure enough to daunt me. I have no regard for truth, no respect for justice, no mercy for the defenseless. My victims are as numerous as the sands of the sea and often as innocent. I never forget and seldom forgive. My name is Gossip.

Any fool can constantly criticize, complain and gossip—most of them do. But, "he who restrains his lips is wise" (Prov. 10:19).

James continues in verse 6: "And the tongue is a fire." The same thing is said once again in the great Book of Proverbs:

A worthless man digs up evil, while his words are a scorching fire.... Like a madman who throws firebrands, arrows and death, so is the man who deceives his neighbor, and says, "was I not joking?" For lack of wood the fire goes out, and where there is no whisperer, contention quiets down. Like charcoal to hot embers and wood to fire, so is a contentious man to kindle strife. The words of a whisperer are like dainty morsels, and they go down into the innermost parts of the body (16:27; 26:18-22).

"The tongue is...the very world of iniquity." The pen may be mightier than the sword, but the tongue is a world of iniquity as well as a sharp sword (Ps. 57:4). It has been the most destructive machine known to man. The tongue is a world of iniquity because it can destroy (Ps. 52:1-4). Listen to the Psalmist:

Why do you boast in evil, O mighty man? The lovingkindness of God endures all day long. Your tongue devises destruction, like a sharp razor, O worker of deceit. You love evil more than good, falsehood more than speaking what is right. You love all words that devour, O deceitful tongue (Ps. 52:1-4).

Words are cheap to say, but no amount of money can buy them back. James says that the tongue "defiles the entire body." The word "defiles" is from the Greek *spilo*, which means "to stain or spot" (Eph. 5:27; II Peter 2:13). This is illustrated by:

Contentious tongues have hindered the work of God a thousand times over. Critical tongues have closed church doors. Careless tongues have broken the hearts and health of many pastors. The sins of the tongue have besmirched the pure white garments of the bride of Christ (Sweeting).

No doubt this is what Jesus meant: "Not what enters into the mouth defiles the man, but what proceeds out of the mouth, this defiles the man" (Matt. 15:11,18).

I was discussing this section of Scripture with a very good pastor-teacher friend of mine. He said that he and his wife where shopping for a bedspread one day. They came across a $200 one that had been reduced in price to $5. The reduction was due to a large stain right in the middle. That stain had ruined the entire value of that beautiful thing. The tongue can be a stain on us that will ruin our total value and worth as a Christian.

The tongue "sets on fire the course of our life." Literally rendered from the Greek, this would be: "Inflaming the course of nature." Indeed, the tongue has destroyed nations and reputations.

The final phrase of verse 6 tells it all: "and is set on fire by hell." This is a reference to Gehenna which Christ described in Matthew 5:22 as "the hell of fire." Zodiates masterfully elaborates on "Gehenna":

> This is a Chaldean word, which was the name of a valley on the southeast of Jerusalem where Moloch, an idol having the form of a bull, dwelt and received into his fiery arms little children thrown there as part of heathen sacrifice. The word actually means "the valley of lamentation," and the Jews so abhorred this place after these horrible sacrifices that, after they had been abolished by King Josiah (II Kings 23:10), they cast into it not only all manner of refuse, but even the dead bodies of animals and of unburied criminals who had been executed. And since fires were always needed to consume dead bodies, the place came to be known as "the gehenna of fire." In the Gospels it occurs some ten times on the lips of the Lord Jesus Christ as describing the place of the future punishment of the wicked, "where their worm dieth not, and the fire is not quenched" (Mark 9:48). This the Lord has made as the symbol of the ever-burning fire to show forth the fate that awaits the ungodly. And as someone has said, "Hell is the rubbish heap of the universe." James is most careful in the presentation of his symbolic figures. He tells us that the evil tongue defiles the whole body. When the whole body is defiled, what good is it but to be thrown on the refuse heap and burned? All evil talk, James says, has its beginning in hell and will cause the whole body, the whole personality, to burn in hell. These are serious words, and we shall do well to heed them. The fire that we start with our tongues has been borrowed from hell and it is going to lead us and others there.

D. The Trainer and the Aminal, 3:7-8. The word "species" in verse 7 means nature (Rom. 1:26). It is used in this context of all animals and man. Nature is denoted as "beasts" or wild, unruly animal; "birds" meaning animals that fly; "reptiles" refers to animals that crawl, therefore includes serpents; "creatures of the sea" refers to those marine animals which inhabit the oceans.

"The human race" or "mankind" has tamed the animals. The force of the Greek might be better stated: the nature of the animal has been domesticated by the nature of the human.

"But" sets up a strong contrast. "No one can tame the tongue." The tongue is the one-of-a-kind creature; namely, *untamable*! Remember that the human author is addressing a primarily Jewish audience in the *Diaspora*.

Yet, with all of his ingenuity expressed in dancing bears, trained seals, talking dolphins, acrobatic birds, snake charming and even penetration into outer space, man has not tamed the tongue! No human can tame the tongue; but God can. "Set a guard, O Lord, over my mouth; keep watch over the door of my lips" (Ps. 141:3). Better a loose *tiger* than a loose *tongue*!

James concludes verse 8 thusly concerning the tongue: "it is a restless evil and full of deadly poison." Two potent pictures are herein discussed. The first, "it is a restless evil." This simply depicts the instability of the tongue. Second, it is "full of deadly poison." Poison-mouthed people destroy just like snakes from a pit who hiss and flick their tongues before they strike. David spoke of them when he wrote, "They sharpen their tongues as a serpent; poison of a viper is under their lips" (Ps. 140:3).

How is the tongue so deadly? There are many ways; but let me give two examples:

1. Character assassination. There are those who seek to discredit and destroy others with their speech. David warns:

> Hear my voice, O God, in my complaint; preserve my life from dread of the enemy. Hide me from the secret counsel of evildoers, from the tumult of those who do iniquity, who have sharpened their tongue like a sword; they aimed bitter speech as their arrow, to shoot from concealment at the blameless; suddenly they shoot at him, and do not fear. They hold fast to themselves an evil purpose; They talk of laying snares secretly; They say "Who can see them?" They devise injustices, saying, "We are ready with a well-conceived plot"; For the inward thought and the heart of man are deep (Ps. 64:1-6).

But God has a way of shooting at the poison-mouth what he or she aims at others:

> But God will shoot at them with an arrow; suddenly they will be wounded. So they will make him stumble; their own tongue is against them; all who see them will shake the head. Then all men will fear and will declare the work of God, and will consider what He has done. The righteous man will be glad in the Lord, and will take refuge in Him; and all the upright in heart will glory (Ps. 64:7-10).

2. Christian cannibalism. This is the second example of how the tongue can be so deadly. What do I mean by "Christian cannibalism"? Listen to

Paul, "But if you bite and devour one another, take care lest you be consumed by one another" (Gal. 5:15). Gossip told often enough will soon be accepted as fact.

Gossip is the crustiest of all sins. Let me illustrate. In Galatians 5:19-21, Paul lists 15 "deeds of the flesh." *Seven* pertain to the tongue! Notice the grouping:

a. Sex sins—immorality, impurity, sensuality.

b. Occult sins—idolatry, sorcery.

c. Tongue sins—enmities, strife, jealousy, outbursts of anger, disputes, dissensions, factions, envyings.

d. Liquor sins—drunkenness, carousings.

God regards sins of the tongue rather seriously!

IV. MATTERS WHICH PROCEED FROM THE MOUTH, 3:9-12

In the third chapter of James, the classic passage on the tongue, the writer brings it all together in verses 9 through 12. There is a contrast (3:9-10) and a contradiction (3:11-12). First, let us consider:

A. The Contrast of Blessing God and Cursing Men, 3:9-10. Oh, the "Knit pickers"—how they wrangle on and on to the disruption of the church. They cause the progress of local churches to come to a veritable standstill and cause the doors to close forever in a community.

They are the New Testament tares, the inexplicable complainers, who make the Lord want to literally retch and ultimately vomit them out of His mouth ((Rev. 3:16). These awful people, who filter throughout our flocks, with their bad mouths, "bless our Lord and Father." Can you believe that! The present tense indicates that they are *always*, or apparently eulogizing God the Father. One would never know that their hearts were rotten to the core with wickedness. They seem so "super spiritual." It reminds me of Judas, the "super saint," that everyone trusted. But he was bad! Can you think of a worse thing than that?

They express pious platitudes about God but "curse men." And to add insult to injury these men they curse "have been made in the likeness of God." This just isn't every man they curse, but literally "those who have been made or have become to be like God." In other words, they harass *believers*! These grumblers and complainers are what Moses called "a mixed multitude" (Exod. 12:38).

It is hard to fathom, but this mixed multitude despised God's gracious gift of the manna. Instead of courteously asking God to "please pass the manna," they were gripers over the manna itself! These, who misused their mouths, angered the Lord in the Book of Numbers (11:1-3) and "the fire of the Lord burned among them and consumed some of the outskirts of the camp...." The Lord spoke to Moses and Aaron in chapter 14 of Numbers saying:

> How long shall I bear with this evil congregation who are grumbling against Me?...Your corpses shall fall in this wilderness, even all your numbered men...who have grumbled against Me (14:27, 29).

Complaints once again angered the Lord and Moses records, "Get away from among this congregation, that I may consume them instantly" (cf. Num. 16:41-50). Dear ones, I would say that misusing the mouth is "playing with fire, "wouldn't you?

The mixed multitude are likened to the tares among the wheat (Matt. 13). Each church has a mixed multitude or a group of tares. These are distinguished by the monumental movements of their mouths as they "make constant waves" by negative speech.

As the mixed multitude of the Old Testament was dissatisfied with the manna, so the tares of the New Testament are disgruntled with the teaching of the Word of God. They therefore complain disparagingly about anything and everything in the church. Nothing seems to please them. Just like the mixed multitude derided Moses and Aaron, the tares speak derogatorily of their pastors and spiritual leaders. (Which, incidentally, when one speaks against God's representative, he speaks against God Himself). The teaching of the Bible, unembellished with gimmicks, is the greatest need of the eleventh hour!

Listen! Receive the Word! Read it! Share it! Live in the good of it! Love it! Experience every word of it! Don't hinder its work with your tongue! Remove yourself from the rank and file of the tares and the mixed multitude (Phil 2:14). May God help each of us to use our tongues to His glory!

Verse 10 records a reeemphasis upon the contrast of blessing God and cussing men. It is a paradox that "from the same mouth come both blessing and cursing." Dr. Robertson explains, "It is a moral incongruity for blessing and cursing to come out of the same mouth." This is like Dr. Jekyll and Mr. Hyde. Say something sweet to a man's face, but behind his back, the jaws of a poison mouth snap shut and with each repeated word crush his reputation like a shark would bite and tear away at a swimmer.

James capsulizes his argument with this simple but ever so enlightening statement: "My brethren, these things ought not to be this way." As a Hebrew himself, perhaps James was making reference to Psalms 62:4,

"...They delight in falsehood; they bless with their mouth, but inwardly they curse." In other words, they profess Christ with their lips but do not possess Him in their hearts. "...such conduct deserves severe reprobation" (Jamison-Fausset-Brown).

Take General George Patton for example. It was said of him that he was violently profane, yet deeply religious. He prayed before battles and knelt beside the beds of the wounded to intercede for them. But, if he was in the presence of a coward or if the tide of war went wrong, he flew into a tirade of blasphemy and intemperate language that would curl the ears of the devil himself. Could this be to what James is referring?

B. The Contradiction by Principles in Nature, 3:11-12. James gives three illustrations from nature to show the contradiction for a professing Christian who does not control his tongue. They are: (1) A fountain with both fresh and bitter water (3:11-12); (2) A fig tree with olive berries (3:12); (3) A vine with figs (3:12). Let us first consider:

1. A fountain with both fresh and bitter water, 3:11-12. The word "fountain" means spring which "sends out" or gushes out water. The point of the illustration is that the source determines the nature of the water (Matt. 12:34). Fresh water doesn't sweeten the bitter; but in contrast— the bitter will spoil the sweet. Inevitably, it seems that the negative mouths have the most influence. One rotten apple spoils the entire barrel of good ones. But, one good apple in a barrel of rotten ones never sweetens the barrel. That is the thrust of James' statement: "Neither can salt water produce fresh." Zodiates illuminates: "A source that yields salt water cannot also yield sweet water from the same opening or hole. There are sources that yield both, but never from the same opening. Thus the mouth that speaks for the Christian heart must be consistent in its behavior toward God and toward His creatures."

2. A fig tree with olive berries, 3:12. The statement is: "Can a fig tree, my brethren, produce olives...." The key is the word "can" which demands a "no" response. The fruit of the tree must be in conformity with the tree. A fig tree must sprout figs, not olives!

3. A vine with figs, 3:12. The fact remains that vines do not produce figs! Vines produce grapes! The root determines the fruit. What is in your heart will be on your lips. May God grip our hearts with these truths.!

V. THE MONSTROSITY THE TONGUE CAN BE

The Bible says: "...their tongue [is] a sharp sword" (Ps. 57:4). "They sharpen their tongues as a serpent..." (Ps. 140:3). The tongue can be a mighty monster!

Dear friend, our words are indicators of what the verdict will be when we stand before God. It will be pay day some day. Listen to this: "For by your words you shall be justified, and by your words you shall be condemned" (Matt. 12:37). Words are powerful! Also who says them carries a lot of weight.

VI. THE METHOD OF TAMING THE TONGUE

A. Acknowledge our need before God (Rom. 3:23).

B. Accept Christ as your personal Saviour (John 1:12).

C. Avoid idle and profane words (Matt. 12:36).

D. Attack gossip whenever it rears its ugly head (Gal. 5:15).

E. Accentuate edifying words (Eph. 4:29-30).

F. Allow the Holy Spirit to control your speech (I Cor. 2:4).

7

The Ways of Wisdom

THE CHAPTER OUTLINED:

I. THE PRESENTATION OF GENUINE WISDOM, 3:13

James inquires, "Who among you is wise and understanding?" To properly comprehend the flow of thought, it is mandatory that one remain cognizant of the fact that this Epistle is meted with a Jewish flavor. Therefore the wisdom under discussion is the Hebrew conception thereof; and, definitely not the Greek.

The words, "wise and understanding" are key in the interpretation of the text. This refers back in the context of chapter 3 to verse 1. It was there that the subject of the Bible teacher was introduced. It was the effective use of his tongue which distinguished him as an adequate or inadequate, superior or inferior expositor of God's Word. Speech, wisdom and understanding are absolutely indispensable to the teacher's success. However, these may be greatly abused as well (I Cor. 1:5, 17; 2:1-3:20).

Dr. Robertson makes a distinction between "wisdom" and "understanding." He states, "*Sophos* is used for the practical teacher (verse 1), *Epistemon* for an expert, a skilled and scientific person with a tone of superiority. In Deuteronomy 1:13, 15; 4:6, the two terms are practically synonyms." One thing is crystal clear, the pastor-teacher must be an expert in his field. His one and only *primary* field is that he demonstrate expertise in the systematic teaching of God's Holy Word based on sound and deep exegetical techniques. The pastor-teacher is not a babysitter, hand-holder, social director or one who goes from house to house sipping tea with his parishioners. He is one who is to study, study, study, study and then teach, teach, teach, teach!

Is it practical for a teacher of the Book to spend most of his ministerial time studying and teaching? Shouldn't he rather be out calling on people or fixing the leak in the faucet, hammering nails in the building, or running the mimeograph, or printing the bulletin, or taking out the trash? I mean, just how much wisdom is it for God to put in His Bible that a pastor should study and teach all the time?

Let's look at some New Testament examples for a moment. The Book of Acts contains some remarkable facts and statistics. We marvel in the reading of them. For example. "...and there were added that *day* about three thousand souls" (2:41); "And the Lord was adding to their number *day by day* those who were being saved" (2:47); "...and the number of the *men* came to be about five thousand" (4:4); "And the word of God *kept on spreading*; and the number of the disciples *continued to increase greatly* in Jerusalem, and a great many of the *priests* were becoming obedient to the faith" (6:7); "And the hand of the Lord was with them, and a large number who believed turned to the Lord" (11:21); "So the churches were being strengthened in the faith, and were increasing in number *daily*" (16:5).

Present-day congregations "hire" a man to do all of the above, and all that does is keep the church small, and send the pastor to an early grave. Who was doing all of those spectacular things in the Book of Acts? It was *NOT* the Apostles for they were simply studying and teaching all day long! The accomplishments of Acts were performed by common, ordinary, garden-variety laymen! When are our churches going to get the point?!

Acts 19:8-10 is a classic passage showing what the *teaching* ministry of the Word of God can achieve. In the text, Luke reports the ministry of Paul in the city of Ephesus. One marginal reading revealed that some ancient manuscripts add the words "from the fifth hour to the tenth" after the sentence, "and took away the disciples, reasoning daily in the school of Tyrannus." Simple mathematical computations demonstrate that the Great Apostle taught these new babes in Christ for five hours a day, every single day for a period of two years. That is a total of some 3,650 hours of teaching. We see clearly why the tenth verse concludes: "so that *all* who lived in Asia heard the Word of the Lord...."

Fantastic indeed, within the span of two years, the occupants of the Roman province of Asia (Ephesus being the capital) heard the good news of salvation. Not everyone became a believer, but everyone was *evangelized!* Who evangelized them? It wasn't Paul because he was in Ephesus teaching five full hours every day; Asia was reached by those whom Paul taught. It was like a prairie fire as believers roared out from Ephesus in the everyday business-world routine sharing their faith in Christ. This all was the fruit of the teaching of a single saint! Man of God, "preach the word; be ready in season and out of season; reprove, rebuke, exhort, with great patience and instruction" (II Tim. 4:2).

This is why it is so very, very practical for the pastor-teacher to be an expert expositor of God's unchanging Word. This necessary expertise in the Bible, James calls "wise and understanding." The reasons are apparent—RESULT!

There is no question about it, preparation precedes presentation, and the greater the presentation, the greater the need for preparation. The word "show" means "to bring to light, to display, to exhibit." As he saturates his thinking by a continual study of the Book, the pastor-teacher will exhibit its truths. He will become a "living letter." This is exactly what Paul means:

You are our letter, written in our hearts, known and read by all men; being manifested that you are a letter of Christ, cared for by us, written not with ink, but with the Spirit of the living God, not on tablets of stone, but on tablets of human hearts (II Cor. 3:2-3).

This display will be "by his good behavior." The preposition indicates source and origin. In other words, the exhibits of conduct are his presentation or wisdom. Christianity is pragmatic. It works. The man who immerses himself in Bible doctrine will exhibit a life style befitting the Master Himself (Col. 2:6; I Peter 2:12).

Without being *trite*, only *true*, actions do speak louder than words. Works are an evidence of faith. He says it again in the word "deeds."

These "deeds" are to be done "in the gentleness of wisdom." "In" reveals that one's works are to be "surrounded by and enveloped" in gentleness. It goes without saying, good *wisdom* is shown by good *works*. This reminds me of Jesus when He said, "Take my heart..." (Matt. 11:29). *Meekness* must never be mistaken for *weakness*. On the contrary, gentleness and meekness is strength under control. Moses was the meekest man who ever lived (Num. 12:3). Yet he killed an Egyptian "heavyweight." Paul also was meek and gentle (II Cor. 10:1). David showed compassion to Saul (I Sam. 24:10). These great men knew something about lowliness of heart. Their strength was controlled. They were not characterized by the asserting of their own merits. Humility is obviously involved. This is not stomping on someone else to "get ahead." It is not a "business-world" mentality of "go, go, go" and a "hustle here and a hustle there." A gentle man doesn't advance himself by self-efforts; but, believe it or not, he advances. Humility is the greatest success secret of the centuries.

However, one of the largest danger areas, which looms before an elder is intellectual pride. Since he studies so much he may think he knows it all. "The pride of knowledge has always been the besetting sin of professional teachers" (Wessel). Therefore, these traits of gentleness are to be "of wisdom." Who is wise? The one who can show meekness. This wisdom is thinking like God thinks, and the only way to do that is to feast on the Scriptures. Yes, much is required of the teacher of the Word. Ross illuminates: "In 1:21 the hearer of the Word was exhorted to receive it with meekness, and now the teacher of the Word is exhorted to manifest this same gracious quality of mind."

II. THE PATTERN OF SPURIOUS WISDOM, 3:14-16

As far as a leader of a congregation is concerned, there is no place for two-faced inconsistency or double-tongued incongruity in his life. Consistency *is* a big deal! If an elder speaks out of "both sides" of his mouth, God help him! Fellow elder, let us be brutally honest about what type of wisdom we are actually manifesting. There is a spurious wisdom and it has a definite pattern as seen in verses 14 through 16. There are three things about false wisdom which James outlines: (A) Its Characteristics, 3:14; (B) It's Cause, 3:15; (C) Its Consequence, 3:16. First of all, please note:

A. Its CHARACTERISTICS, 3:14. The word "but" sets up a strong contrast between the true wisdom of verse 13 and the false wisdom of verse 14. The characteristics of spurious wisdom are:

1. It has bitter jealousy. "Bitter jealousy" describes a pastor-teacher who has pride in his knowledge or achievements. Paul reinforces, "... knowledge makes arrogant, but love edifies" (I Cor. 8:1). By application, we can see any man, who, for any reason, exhibits a bitter jealousy. This is one who is always trying to prove he is better than someone else. Therefore he is critical of those who "threaten" his super-inflated ego and tries to elevate himself by verbally putting others down. This is his deranged way of self-reinforcement. He thinks that he is so wise, but James says that his wisdom is spurious. The word "jealous" is from the Greek *zelon* from which we derive the English "zealous." Zealousness is the ardent and passionate pursuit of something. In the New Testament, it is used in a good sense (John 2:17) as well as a bad sense, as here, and in Acts 5:17. The problem-oriented person, who is plagued with jealousy, is zealous in his pursuit of passionately putting other people down.

The word "bitter" is from a root word which means "to cut." This jealous person cuts others like a knife which penetrates into someone's side and is then twisted. What a horribly, infectious evil the bitterly jealous pastor can perpetrate. By the very nature of his status in the body of believers, people are prone to believe him when he spreads negativism about others. A poison-mouthed pastor should be romoved from his position. False wisdom:

2. Has selfish ambition. "Selfish ambition" is really only one word in the Greek. The literal idea is "strife or factious." This depicts the elder who proceeds in raising dissensions in order to advance himself in the eyes of others. His personal ambition is all that matters to him; therefore, he is always at strife with anything or anyone who stands in his way. This kind of person is easily recognizable because he is never at peace with his fellow man. Barclay offers:

> ...you can tell what a man's relations with God are by looking

at his relations with his fellow men. If a man is at variance with his fellow men, if he is a quarrelsome, competitive, argumentative, trouble-making creature, he may be a diligent church attender, he may even be a church office-bearer, but he is not a man of God. ... If a man is distant from his fellow men it is good proof that he is distant from God; if he is divided from his fellow men, he is divided from God.

He is like a bumper sticker I saw once: "Feel far from God? Guess who moved!" Spurious wisdom also:

3. Is arrogant. James adds, "...do not be arrogant...." The word "arrogant" is a compound word in the original composed of two words, a preposition "against" and a verb meaning "to brag." It literally connotes "bragging against." This pastor-teacher has such high regard for himself; he is so arrogant, that he brags of himself continually even to the injury of other people. We learned in verse 13 that genuine wisdom is gentle and humble. Arrogant wisdom is counterfeit. The fourth characteristic of superficial wisdom is that it is a:

4. Lie against the truth. James has a definite reason for exposing the arrogant wisdom for it is simply a belligerent "lie against the truth" (*pseudesthe kata tes aletheias*). In other words, these teachers contradicted their profession of wisdom by means of their conduct. They were living a lie and therefore were walking contradictions. Contradictions of what, you might ask. They were completely contradictory in their arrogance since true wisdom is meek, gentle and humble of heart. Fellow elders, you and I need to evaluate the motives of our hearts in the light of this piece of revelation recorded in James. Spurious wisdom is exposed as to:

B. Its CAUSE, 3:15. The false wisdom of the arrogant teacher "is not that which comes down from above." This should be obvious to the student of James, since it has been stated before that all genuine wisdom comes from God Himself (1:5, 17). God is not the source of the wisdom of the bad-mouthed teacher. On the contrary, the source is:

1. Earthly. "Earthly" means that man produces this type of wisdom. Any teaching or teacher who does not have Biblical warrant therefore produces a homocentric perspective. This would encompass *all* human philosophy. Colossians 2:8 contributes: "See to it that no one takes you captive through philosophy and empty deception, according to the tradition of men, according to the elementary principles of the world, rather than according to Christ."

Human philosophies are at variance with the Biblical text. Let's cite some examples. Theistic evolution or evolution per se is opposed to the first two chapters of Genesis. The inherent goodness of man contradicts the Bible's teaching of total depravity (Rom. 3:10-12). Penal rehabilitation never reformed anyone. Only the new birth can change a life (John 3:1-21). Humanistic philosophy postulates that the many religious systems will get a man to heaven like so many spokes on a wheel, which all lead to the same place; namely, the hub. The Scriptures say there is only *one* way to heaven (John 14:6); namely, the Person of Jesus Christ. Well, so much for earthly wisdom, which is also:

2. Natural. "Natural" is from the Greek and literally means "soul-ishness." We derive our English word "psychology" from *psuchike*. Dr. Strauss assists us in seeing the contrast of the natural to the spiritual as distinguished in I Corinthians 2:14-15. He says:

> The unregenerate man at his best is governed by his own lusts and is described by Jude as "sensual, having not the Spirit" (Jude 19). The wisdom that is earthly and sensual has as its aim the glory of man. Whenever a Christian employs tactics it can only lead him into difficulty. False wisdom belongs to the baser nature in man. It does not come from the Spirit of God.

The one who does what comes naturally; namely, the one who is guided by his glands is described in I Corinthians 2:14; "But a natural man does not accept the things of the Spirit of God; for they are foolishness to him, and he cannot understand them, because they are spiritually appraised." Dr. James L. Boyer has noted four things about the natural man. I have paraphrased them accordingly, in that he has:

1. A limited nature—his spirit is dead and therefore cannot respond to God.

2. A prejudiced disposition—the things of God are not welcome in his life.

3. A distorted judgment—the things of God are moronic to him.

4. Inadequate abilities—he lacks the necessary equipment to examine spiritual things. He is like a blind man in an art gallery, like a deaf man at a symphony.

Not having the necessary equipment for proper perception is somewhat like a small child. Little Petunia, a six year old, complained, "Mommie, I've got a tummy ache." "That's because your stomach is empty," her mother replied. That evening in church services, the pastor remarked that he had a splitting headache. Petunia perked up and said to her mother:

"That's because his head is empty. He would feel better if he had something in it." Earthly wisdom is described by James in a third manner as:

3. Demonic. "Demonic" is from the original *daimoniodes*. In other words, the man who says he is wise and his life style contradicts it, then his wisdom has its source in demons. It is shocking, but true, demons have their own doctrines which can be camouflaged in the cloak of the church. A preacher doesn't necessarily have to wear his collar backwards, with his theology to match, to espouse deviate doctrines from the mainline Biblical point of view. Even if a teaching denies only a small portion of truth, it is of demons. Demons spread false doctrine among the things to which the people of God are attending (I Tim. 4:1-5; 5:8; II Cor. 11:13-15; Rev. 12:9). Demonic direction will *always* be away from the body of truth; that is, the faith. Those who follow demonic delusions depart from the faith, not their faith (which the Scriptures say is impossible to lose), but the faith and belief in the Bible (I Tim. 4:1; II John 9; Acts 20:29-30). Error is an insidious thing, and a pastor-teacher who has deceived himself into believing that he has wisdom, when in reality, his wisdom is earthly, will inadvertently lead his people astray.

Blatantly, there is demonic deception on every hand. Wilbur Smith warns:

> I am becoming more and more convinced that many of the awful and blasphemous teachings that are now found in the literature of our day, indeed, in some of the most widely circulated and highly praised books of our generation have been prompted... by evil spirits.

One of the most effective "selling points" of Satan is to confuse us as to what genuine wisdom is and what it is not. These powerful summations of William Barclay help clear the confusion:

> James then describes this arrogant and bitter wisdom in its effects. The most notable thing about it is that it issues in disorder. That is to say, instead of bringing people together, it drives them apart. Instead of producing peace, it produces strife. Instead of producing a fellowship it produces a disruption in personal relationships. There is a kind of person who is undoubtedly clever; he has an acute brain and a skillful tongue; but his effect in any committee, in any church, in any group, is to cause trouble, to drive people apart, to foment strife, to make trouble, to disturb personal relationships. It is a sobering thing to remember that what that man possesses is devilish rather than divine, and that such a man in engaged in Satan's work and not in God's work. It may well be said that all forces which make for division are forces which are against the will of God, and which advance the cause of the devil.

The wisdom of this world is charming, solicitous and elusive to some, but ever so destructive. Which brings us to:

C. Its CONSEQUENCE, 3:16. The above quotation by Barclay has already given to us some pertinent information on the consequence of earthly wisdom. But, James spells it out most gravely. He solemnizes, "For where jealousy and selfish ambition exist, there is disorder and every evil thing." "Jealousy" and "selfish ambition" have already been dealt with in verse 14 above.

Its consequence is "disorder." This word denotes several things such as "disturbance, confusion, instability" and even "anarchy." When this disruptive condition is extant, you can be assured that the Holy Spirit is not present. It is apparent, therefore, that disunited and disputatious church business meetings are verifications that God is not there. It is just like Paul said, "For God is not a God of confusion but of peace, as in *all* the churches of the saints" (I Cor. 14:33).

Spurious wisdom also results in "every evil thing," which literally is "every worthless practice." The word "thing" is the Greek *pragma* of which our word "pragmatic" is the transliteration. It denotes the product of experience. In this particular instance, it is a constantly bad experience. This is the result of wrong attitudes toward others.

Dear reader, what type of wisdom are you manifesting? Before the Lord, acknowledge any counterfeits that you are tolerating. Frankly attribute them to their real cause as merely earthly, sensual and demonic. Contrasted to this false wisdom is:

III. THE PRODUCTION OF GENUINE WISDOM, 3:17-18

This "for sure" wisdom stems from God, to the hearts of pastor-teachers, in response to their faith. It also "reflects God-like characteristics as its fruits" (Rosscup). In this light, please consider:

A. Its CHARACTERISTICS, 3:17.

1. It is from above. The source and origin of genuine wisdom is "from above." The term is used in John 3:1-7 as well as in James' very own epistle (1:17). Therefore genuine wisdom is not physical or earthly, but spiritual. This is simply a spiritual relationship and a contact with God through Christ. Therefore there is an intimacy with God Himself. Until a man is born from above, he cannot know and experience wisdom from above.

The Spirit of God effects the spiritual birth (John 3:8) and is complemented by the Bible as the assisting agent (Eph. 5:26). Our part is simply to believe on the finished work of Jesus Christ on the cross in substitution for us (Rom. 10:9-10). It is imperative to be born from above to live forever and experience His wisdom. Wessel relates, "It is the gift of God; it is practical wisdom, wisdom that preserves unity and peace."

2. It is pure. "Pure" means "undefiled" (Ropes). This quality should spring from within a man where Christ indwells. Christ alone can produce this (Gal. 5:22-23). This demonstrates that there are no false motives in heavenly wisdom. There is no selfish ambition in it to *any* degree!

3. It is peaceable. This certainly is in contradistinction to the ominous entourage of deadly poison which is characteristic of a pastor (or *anyone* else for that matter) who is engrossed with worldly wisdom (I Cor. 1:20). The peaceable man is the opposite of the one whose obstreperous mouth is incessantly stirring up trouble. "Peaceable" is the quality of a heart which is rightly related to the Lord. Heavenly wisdom:

4. Is gentle. The word "gentle" is not the same word translated "gentleness" in verse 13. It is an adjective and appears four times in the *Koine New Testament* (I Tim. 3:3; Titus 3:2; here in 3:17 and I Peter 2:18). The connotation is that of "equitableness," which issues in fairness. The man whose wisdom ensues from above, is a man whose activities are more in the *spirit* of the law than in the *letter* of the law. ·

Wise is the man who is ever-presently aware that he has been dealt with by God not with the *letter* of the law, which would send him to hell, but in *grace* through Christ. In the experience of my ministry, it seems that the *grossest* of *sinners*, after conversion, result in the most *gracious* of *saints*. He who has been pardoned from the most, usually is the most gracious to others. He knows what forgiveness is all about. This is wisdom! This is the wisdom from above, which also:

5. Is reasonable. "Reasonable" means "easily approachable" with requests. This is a mandatory quality for the pastor-teacher if he is to be used of the Lord. A man who spends more time studying the Word of God is a man who becomes very wise. When people hear him speak, they immediately discern that he is a man who spends time with the Lord. They want to approach him and ask things of him. Wherever the life of a man is explainable only in the terms of God—other men are seeking that man for help and counsel. It is readily apparent that his wisdom is from above because he virtually *lives* in the Scriptures.

6. Full of mercy. The concept of being "full of mercy" connotes the one who is more than willing to help. It is a translucent pity for others who are without God in their lives. You and I who love the Lord, and who have been recipients of His mercy to us, should assuage the hurts of others. Our faces should be composed in the benign, even compassionate expression of those who are absolutely certain of God's goodness and kindness. This same benevolence which He has bestowed upon us should be transferred to others. Coupled with this wisdom from above is:

7. Good fruit. "Good fruit" is the result of good seed. The good seed is the Word of God which has saturated the one who produces good fruit. How refreshingly different this is from the calamitous clamorings which James has been previously writing about, which end is a lugubrious demise. The elliptically adamant mouth produces the bad fruit ·of dementia because the seed has been gossip and not God's good Word. But the gorgeous amenities that surround the life of the one who is *in* the Great Book is something to behold. This type of person is known by his beatific smile which makes happy wreaths of the face itself. Certainly this is heavenly wisdom in its finest form. Finally, let us learn of:

B. Its CONSEQUENCE, 3:18. Verse 18 is a delightful one: "And the seed whose fruit is righteousness is sown in peace by those who make peace."

"The seed whose fruit is righteousness" would be better rendered "fruit of righteousness." This "is sown in peace." It is a present passive indicative from the verb *speiro* which means "to sow." The lesson from the grammar is most pertinent. This one's amicable life is *habitually* sowing the seed of peace. He has so much Bible doctrine in his frontal lobe, that everywhere he goes, he passively and even inadvertently scatters the seeds of peace. He is "Johnny Peace-seed." Jesus calls him a "peacemaker" (Matt. 5:9). Dr. Robertson blesses us with:

> The seed which bears the fruit is sown, but James catches up the metaphor of *Karpos* (fruit) from verse 17. Only in peace is the fruit of righteousness found ... Only those who act peaceably are entitled to peace.

With all of the above "input," how easy it will be for all of us to evaluate what type of wisdom we are reflecting. The challenge is to live in the therapeutic stream of God's Word and to think like He thinks.

Who Controls Your Life?

THE CHAPTER OUTLINED:

I. The **CAUSE** Behind the Struggle, 4:1-5
   A. Strife, 4:1
   B. An Unnecessary Threefold Lack, 4:2
   C. Unanswered Prayer, 4:3
   D. Results in Spiritual Adultery, 4:4
   E. Spiritual Unyieldedness, 4:5

II. The **CURE** for the Struggle, 4:6-11
   A. The **AVAILABILITY** of Grace, 4:6
   B. The **APPROPRIATION** of Grace, 4:7-11

I. THE CAUSE BEHIND THE STRUGGLE, 4:1-5

James has just preached to the preacher in chapter 3 about the use of his tongue as he taught among the ancients. James also instructed these pastor-teachers concerning the differences between genuine and spurious wisdom. In order to cover all the bases, James now addresses himself to the members of the local churches (synagogues, in the first century). Everyone, from the top down, is susceptible to sins of the tongue. In verses 1 through 5 the human author blasts away at 5 major problems among the members.

Contrasted to the tranquil life style defined in 3:18, some of the saints in the *diaspora* were characterized by inward strivings and outward wranglings to satisfy *fleshly* desires, by intimate cravings after pleasures of the *world* and by *demonic* dispositions (cf. v. 7; 3:15). In the words of Rosscup:

> Though there were gratifications of their lusts, there were also many bitter disappointments and souring frustrations. They were hollow people, and sick of the grievous boredom of life without fulfillment. Their shams of religious pretense did not bring contentment, and their prayers seemed to fall back upon their heads without effect.

This warfare was caused by the *flesh*. The flesh's production was diagnosed by James, when he asked two searching questions of his Jewish brethren: (1) "What is the source of quarrels and conflicts among you?" (2) "Is not the source your pleasures that wage war in your members?" Breaking this down under the expository microscope we see that the lust of the flesh caused:

A. Strife, 4:1. It is as true then as it is now that peace among Christians is much needed and long overdue. How strange that so many believers are at variance with themselves and others in light of the legacy that the Lord has left; namely, peace (John 14:27; James 3:18).

What is the source or origin of strife? This is an excellent question since all belligerence is only symptomatic of something deeper. Therefore, rather than just treating the symptoms, James goes right to the heart of the problem in his interrogation. What is the source of:

1. Quarrels. "Quarrels" is from the Greek *polemoi* and indicates private fights, battles, bickerings and squabbles between individual members of the congregation. This is a terrible thing! There seems to be a corrosive element that characterized malcontents in churches. I have seen people leave a church where there was a "spiritual giant," who taught the Word of

God in all of its power. They left over some petty, personal preference or over policy or over a quarrel with another member. They leave and go awry and flounder from church to church, never satisfied and never agreeing on anything. Nothing ever seems to suit them. This seems to have been the problem between Paul and Demas. Demas faded out. Paul says, "For Demas, having loved this present world, has deserted me..." (II Tim. 4:10). He abondoned Paul and went to Thessalonica. He maintained the friendship of this world. He allowed the world to creep into his life. This resulted in a falling-out with Paul and Demas "headed for the hills." His forsaking Paul was the one thing that revealed his true colors. People who quarrel and leave the church—what does that tell us? John answers with these expletives: "They went out from us, but they were not really of us; for if they had been of us, they would have remained with us; but they went out, in order that it might be shown that they are not of us" (I John 2:19). What is the source of:

2. Conflicts. The word "conflicts" denotes an entire campaign of hassles. Rather than just a *fray* between individuals, this is a *foray* among the whole membership! When a conflict like this arises, all the factions of the church come out of the wood-work. It is a "show-down" at the congregational business meeting corral. I know of a case where the color of carpet was up for grabs. One faction in the group wanted blue and the other schism wanted red. At Sunday's business meeting it was to be settled by vote. During the week the town's phone lines were humming as each group called their supporters to instigate a voting-block rally at the impending meeting. People showed up at church who had not been there for years! Well, the "reds" won and the "blues" promptly stood to their feet and left en masse. The church was split over the color of the carpet. They were divided over a personal preference. Whether or not it was a Bible issue never entered anyone's mind! The church was incredibly weakened and Satan scored a point. The local church was the real loser.

Indeed, the source of conflicts and quarrels is "your pleasures" (*ek ton hedonon humon*). Our English word "hedonism" (*hedonon*) carries the idea of making pleasure the sole purpose in life by gratifying all of the baser instincts and dispositions of the heart. Note in I Corinthians 15:32 where the motto of Hedonism is recorded: "Let us eat and drink, for tomorrow we die." Hedonistic tendencies are described by Paul as those who are "...lovers of pleasure rather than lovers of God" (II Tim. 3:4). The one outside of Christ is guided by his glands. Titus 3:3 says, "For we also once were foolish ourselves, disobedient, deceived, enslaved to various lusts and pleasures, spending our life in malice and envy, hateful, hating one another."

When Christians are contentious it is because their pleasures "wage war" in their lives. "Wage war" is from a very vivid military word in the Greek. It comes from a root word, *strateuo*, which means "to do military service, serve as a soldier" (Arndt and Gingrich) as in Luke 3:14; I Corinthians 9:7 and II Timothy 2:4. It is used in a figurative sense here and in I Peter 2:11, "Beloved, I urge you as aliens and strangers to abstain from fleshly lusts, which wage war against the soul." Needless to say that believers can be besieged by an entire army of lusts. Soldiers of lust beleaguer the soul.

It is my humble opinion that our churches need to reenact the lost art of church discipline which is presented in Matthew 18:15-20. This is greatly neglected, and it would protect us against the armies of evil which lurk latently in our lives if we would only practice it. The life of the local church would be greatly enhanced if immediate discipline was in vogue to regulate its affairs. By the authority of the Lord Jesus Christ, the local church *has* been delegated the responsibility to discipline its own (I Cor., chap. 5; Titus 3:10; II Thess. 3:6-15; I Tim. 5:20; Gal. 6:1). If just one divisive argumentation among saints could be avoided in any church by including this discussion in my book, then it was worthwhile.

Here are the grounds and procedures of New Testament church discipline:

(1) Matters of unresolved personal contention (Matt. 18:15-17).

(a) An individual seeing his brother sinning has the personal responsibility to admonish him in love (Gal. 6:1; James 5:19-20).

(b) If remedial action does not result, the sinning brother should be confronted by two or three others, who will bear witness to the admonition and its acceptance or rejection by the errant brother.

(c) If the sinning brother rejects the admonition witnessed by the two or three, the matter is brought to the whole church for further admonishment.

(d) Refusal to accept the admonition from the church will result in withdrawal of fellowship.

(2) The Scriptures provide (I Cor. 6:1-11) that matters of contention between believers should be settled by church action, not by litigation. Failure to do this or to abide by the decision of the church is grounds for discipline.

(3) The Scriptures reveal several categories of offense requiring disciplinary action:

(a) Immorality—I Corinthians 5:11.

(b) Difficulties between individual members—Matthew 18:15-17;

I Corinthians 5:5-6.

(c) Disorderly conduct—II Thessalonians 3:6-11.

(d) Being an unproductive gossiper—II Thessalonians 3:11-12.

(e) Divisiveness—Romans 16:17-18; Titus 3:9-10.

(f) Failure to esteem spiritual leaders properly—I Thessalonians 5:12-14; Hebrews 13:17.

(g) Gross sins—I Timothy 5:20.

(h) Covetousness, idolatry, abusive speech, drunkenness and swindling—I Corinthians 5:11.

(i) False teaching—I Timothy 1:20; II Timothy 2:17-18.

(j) Divorce for reasons other than the Biblical grounds as set forth in Matthew 19:9.

(4) Purposes in discipline.

(a) For the correction of the disobedient—II Thessalonians 3:14.

(b) For the unity and purity of the church—Ephesians 5:11; I Corinthians 5:6-7.

(c) For the preservation of the testimony and witness of the church—I Corinthians 5:12.

(d) For the ultimate, remedial purpose of restoring the errant one to fellowship once again—I Corinthians 5:5.

It goes without saying that had these believers, under discussion in James' letter, put into action the above disciplinary processes, their factious and disruptive affairs would have been nonexistent. But, nonetheless, their fleshly lusts caused:

B. An Unnecessary Threefold Lack, 4:2. In parallelism, James portrays three things in which his Jewish compatriots lack—the first is:

1. "You lust." This is the same word used in James 1:14 and 15. The word connotes to passionately crave in an illicit manner. These people were hotly desiring but were unrequited and unsatiated. To wrongfully long for what one does not have or for what someone else has is a primary reason for quarrels and conflicts.

This yearning is the habit of life of the one in question since the present tense is utilized. But these "do not have." That is the irony of greed—to passionately crave and not have! In God's plan, the man who craves everything ends up with nothing; whereas the man who illicitly desires nothing, ends up with everything.

"So you commit murder." This is the result of a man who wants what another possesses but cannot acquire it. His envying is just as bad as murder. Even words can kill as well as habitual hating, as John has so tersely told us (I John 3:15). Nothing is more counter-productive.

2. The second lack, which is readily apparent is: "you are envious."

This is our familiar word for jealous. You recall that it was a condition which plagued the pastor-teacher with the super-inflated ego back in 3:14 and 16. Now it is infecting the people. Even this jealous person "cannot obtain." Oh, the jealous people, who are so threatened by the status or possessions of someone else, that they begin a tirade of tearing them down. Somehow, in their deteriorated mentality, they believe that by discrediting those of whom they are ever-so jealous, that some will think higher of them. This is a man who is enthralled with extreme jealousy since he is unsuccessful in obtaining that which is of merit in others. What does he do? James answers, "you fight and quarrel," from the same root words as are in verse 1. Obviously, the first and second lacks are directly attributable to the exercising of wrong motives and methods for obtaining one's needs and wants.

Paul said that prayer is the correct method. "Be anxious for nothing, but in everything by prayer and supplication with thanksgiving let your requests be made known to God. And the peace of God, which surpasses all comprehension, shall guard your hearts and your minds in Christ Jesus" (Phil. 4:6-7).

Christ postulates, "Do not be anxious then, saying, 'What shall we eat?' or 'What shall we drink?' or, 'With what shall we clothe ourselves?' For all these things the Gentiles eagerly seek; for your heavenly Father knows that you need all these things. But seek first His Kingdom, and His righteousness; and all these things shall be added to you. Therefore do not be anxious for tomorrow; for tomorrow will care for itself. Each day has enough trouble of its own" (Matt. 6:31-33).

3. These above passages reveal the third lack of these brethren. They did not have because they did not ask. Jesus said, "Ask, and it shall be given to you..." (Matt. 7:7). The difference is very simple to discern. James 4:2-3 is man's direct seeking. This is the human way. Matthew 6:33 is the indirect seeking which is God's method. Ropes adds,

> Make the service of God your supreme end, and then your desires will be such as God can fulfill in answer to your prayer.

Human passions also cause:

C. Unanswered Prayer, 4:3. These Hebrew converts to Christ manifested fleshly attitudes. This exhibition is diametrically opposed to faith. Therefore, they did not "receive" the answers they were seeking for their prayers. "James has already said that the man who prays without faith cannot expect anything from the Lord (1:6). God will not tolerate the effrontery of men who selfishly seek to take advantage of Him" (Rosscup).

James is not faulting them for *what* they ask, but *why* they ask. The motives of the heart are uppermost to the successful prayer life. Prayer is to be according to the will of God, not the lust of the flesh (I John 5:14-15; Ps. 37:4; I Tim. 6:17). Fleshly desire:

D. Results in Spiritual Adultery, 4:4. Remember that James is writing to Jews who have found fulfillment of their messianic hope in Jesus Christ. They would therefore be very well acquainted with the Old Testament. James takes advantage of this and uses an Old Testament concept which would be quite familiar to the Jews, that of spiritual adultery (for example, Isa. 1:21; 54:5; 57:7-9; Hosea 1:2; 4:12).

Spiritual adultery is committed when the Christian is in love with the world. The one who is in love with the world is "an enemy of God." There is no more formidable enemy than God. Sometimes friendship with the world is seemingly innocent and most subtle. Worldliness is an *attitude* and it is an *affection*. The believers who practice affinity, with this present system of evil, are "adulteresses." This is unfaithfulness to God. Jeremiah 3:20 contributes, " 'Surely, as a woman treacherously departs from her lover, so you have dealt treacherously with Me, O house of Israel,' declares the Lord."

God communicates to man in language with which he can identify, relate to and understand. It seems as if sex, love and marriage have transcultural similarities in all societies. Therefore Christ compares the church to a man's bride (Eph. 5:25). Listen to this: "...for I betrothed you to one husband, that to Christ I might present you as a pure virgin" (II Cor. 11:2).

Therefore the Lord is "jealous for you with a godly jealousy" (II Cor. 11:2). This makes sense when one understands the depths of the psychology of man. Let me explain. Matthew 6:24 reads: "No one can serve two masters; for either he will hate the one and love the other, or he will hold to one and despise the other. You cannot serve God and Mammon." Let me say it this way; man has a one track heart. He cannot love opposites. God will have all of you or none of you simply because He wishes to protect you from yourself. John tells his readers to stop loving the world (cf. I John 2:15-17). John aptly records this principle in the words of Christ.: "If you were of the world, the world would love its own; but because you are not of the world, but I chose you out of the world, therefore the world hates you" (John 15:19). John registers more of the same:

> I have given them Thy word; and the world has hated them,
> because they are not of the world. I do not ask Thee to take them
> out of the world, but to keep them from the evil one. They are not
> of the world, even as I am not of the world (John 17:14-16).

The Lord is not espousing *isolation* from the world; but, *insulation*. A ship floating in the water is most enjoyable. But, when the water is in the ship, then everyone bails out in life rafts.

It is a *real* world, and you and I are *in* it but not *of* it. The libertine advocates, "You only go round once, so grab all the gusto you can get." The ascetic pleads for retreating into a monastic barrenness. The legalist maintains a list to which he must conform and the slightest aberration, as they define it, is horrible. But the Lord says that the Christian is to be a pungent catalyst for change *in* the world (Matt. 5:13-16).

The Biblical use of the term "world" does not primarily refer to a globe, which hangs in outer space on nothing, upon which men inhabit. It is the organization or system of unregenerate humanity which has removed God and has relegated Satan to its headship. This is why, friendship with the world is whoredom of the worst order. Therefore it is not a question of what you *have* but what *has* you (Rom. 12:1-2; I Cor. 6:12).

Lust of the flesh carries the primary connotation of sexual promiscuity in the minds of many. Granted, lust of the flesh can be manifested sexually, but it has so many other disclosures such as those which James picturesquely portrays. He seems to major in the misuses of the mouth, as lust of the flesh, as well as five other displays of a carnal heart in 4:1-5. The fifth cause of fleshly lust is:

E. Spiritual Unyieldedness, 4:5. Verse 5 adduces "a further reason why a Christian cannot be a friend of the world" (Wessel). The term "Scriptures" refers to the Old Testament wherein God has continuously made clear that "He jealously desires the spirit which He has made to dwell in us." "God is a jealous God [cf. Exod. 20:5; 34:14; Deut. 32:16; Zech. 8:2; I Cor. 10:22], and hence he will not tolerate divided allegiance. No specific Old Testament passage contains the words of this verse, but many passages express a similar sentiment" (Wessel).

The word "spirit" is key to the understanding of what is being said. From *pneuma* the English derives such words as pneumatic, pneumatometer, pneumococcus and pneumonia. The primary meaning of *pneuma* is air, wind or spirit. Believe it or not, dear reader, *pneuma* in verse 5 makes it one of the most difficult verses in the entire Bible to interpret. Even old Erasmus said, "There is a wagon load of viewpoints here." Does *pneuma* refer to the Holy Spirit or to the human spirit? I believe that verse 5 has the human spirit in perspective and it is that same spirit in which God desires to dwell.

Unfortunately the human spirit can be defiled. II Corinthians 7:1 enjoins: "Therefore, having these promises, beloved, let us cleanse ourselves from all defilement of flesh and spirit, perfecting holiness in the fear of God." The spirit, man's most intimate part, can be allured by alien attractions. God is jealous for a human spirit, which is pure, undefiled and uncontaminated from the world (Exod. 20:5). Yieldedness to the Spirit's control is mandatory (Rom. 6:16-18). After perusal of the cause behind the struggle of believers, let us consider:

II. THE CURE FOR THE STRUGGLE, 4:6-11

The cure for the struggle simply set forth, is God's enablement (Eph. 3:20-21). This super-strength is seen in:

A. The AVAILABILITY of Grace, 4:6. Verse 6 succinctly states, "But He gives a greater grace." "But" sets up the contrast. "Greater grace" is in contrast to the great lust of the flesh which was elaborated upon in verses 1 through 5. But God's grace is greater than all our sin, for by it we are saved (Eph. 2:8-9). Yes, the pull of the world is great; but, the grace of God is greater (Rom. 6:14). "Grace," *charis* in Greek, is my favorite Bible word. Why? Because it is God's giving to me what I do not deserve. It is His unmerited favor bestowed upon me. Here, in the state of California, the citizens are allowed to order personalized license plates. The Greek word for grace appears on mine. Praise Him forever for grace!

Grace is His supernatural means whereby you and I can live the Christian life. God has always been willing to deal, in an unmerited manner, with man. The Lord is ready, with divine enablement, to assist you and me to please Him. Yes, the Bible records the immense failure of man (Rom. 3:23; 5:12; James 4:5); but, it also speaks of God's secret and supply of victory. It is:

> **God's**
> **Riches**
> **At**
> **Christ's**
> **Expense.**

Verse 6 continues: "Therefore it says, 'God is opposed to the proud, but gives grace to the humble.' " This is a direct quotation from Proverbs 3:34. If there is something that God implicitly disdains, it is pride and a perverse mouth. The words of Proverbs 8:13 are fearful: "The fear of the

Lord is to hate evil; pride and arrogance and the evil way, and the perverted mouth, I hate." Ouch!

Verse 6 is deeply poignant. Let us delve into it more deeply. The word "proud" appears in various forms throughout the Scriptures (I Peter 5:5; Mark 7:22; Luke 1:51; Rom. 1:30; II Tim. 3:2). It is composed of two words: one, a preposition, meaning "above"; and, a verb denoting "to show." The connotation is that of an arrogant, haughty and disdainful individual who "shows oneself above others." This person has delusions of grandeur. He is like the young girl who went to her pastor and confessed that she feared she had incurred the sin of pride revealing itself in vanity. "What makes you think that?" asked the minister. "Because every morning, when I look into the mirror I think how beautiful I am." The reassuring reply was: "Never fear, my girl; that isn't a sin, it is only a mistake."

Allow me to put the fear of God in the both of us for a moment. "God is opposed to the proud." That is a strong statement and it is even stronger in the Greek which compounds its seriousness. The word "opposed" is a military term. It depicts a full armada, decorated with regalia flowing and fortified to the hilt, standing in combat array, ready to do battle. When that kind of word is used of God, back off, now! I would rather take on a mountain of muscle and a thousand-man mob than God. A humble heart is needed and:

B. The APPROPRIATION of Grace is the Cure, 4:7-11. Most everyone is aware that the Old Testament contains the Ten Commandments (Exod. 20:1-17). But, dear reader, there are ten imperatives in James 4:7-11. An imperative is a command and when it is used with the aorist (simple past) tense it carries the idea of urgency. The following ten directives are important always and in all ways:

1. Submission to God, 4:7. "Submit therefore to God." The term "submit" means "to place or rank under." It is used of a wife's submission to her husband (Eph. 5:22; I Peter 3:1). It is obligatory for every creature, who draws breath, to rank under the Lord! It is the first logical step for any of us to take, in the establishment of a relationship, with God. The way up in Christianity is down with self before the Lord. This is the principle of God's blessing (4:6). The *how* of this is seen in the second imperative, which is:

2. Resistance to the devil, 4:7. I used to think that Satan's main territory of operation was where the drunks and down and out congregated. Why would Satan spend time in that vicinity? He already *owns* those people. The devil aims his guns at the Christian and fires away with all barrels. This is graphically portrayed in C.S. Lewis' great piece of literature, *The Screwtape Letters.* Somehow, I surmise, that Satan spends more time in church services than he does anywhere else.

It goes without saying that Christians are locked in mortal combat with demonic hordes (Eph. 6:10-20). Therefore we must "resist the devil." This means to take a stand against him. The offense is twofold: (a) To saturate your mind with God's Word (Matt. 4:4; I Tim. 4:5; II Tim. 3:16; I Peter 1:24-25; II Peter 1:21); (b) to maintain an invigorating life of prayer (John 15:7; I John 5:14-15).

The reason for Satan's success in neutralizing the testimony of the church in the world is Biblical illiteracy and prayerlessness. But, when individual Christians utilize the above weapons, the result is Satan "will flee from you." As Peter says, "But resist him, firm in your faith..." (I Peter 5:9). This is how Satan takes it on the chin for the final count. The only way to be firm in the faith is to literally live in the sphere of God's Word. The third imperative has to do with:

3. Drawing near to God, 4:8 Why are so many who profess Christ so satisfied to live lives in the same old way every single day? Perhaps it is because imperative number two, above, is not practiced. The unsubmitted Christian *will* be defeated by Satan. Satan uses *pride* (I Tim. 3:6). On the one hand the voice of humility sweetly admits, "I can do it by God's grace." On the other hand, the voice of pride adamantly advertises, "I would rather do it myself!" This is what James is announcing in verse 7—put yourself under God in order to stay on top of the devil! Flee the baser drives of the heart as did Joseph, and "draw near to God." When we draw near to God in sweet submission, we will *NOT* speak evil of others.

"Draw near to God" is the prerequisite, "and He will draw near to you." There is an important principle here. God responds to you as much as you respond to Him. God *blesses* as much as you will *believe* Him. In the words of Christ,"...Be it done to you according to your faith" (Matt. 9:29).

Just how can an individual draw near to God? This is answered in imperative number four; which is:

4. Cleansing of the hands, 4:8. "Cleanse your hands." Dr. Robertson comments on its meaning which is "to cleanse, from dirt in a ritual sense" (Exod. 30:19-21; Mark 7:3, 19). Here it is figurative, as in Psalm 24:4. This is the method of drawing near to God as it is coupled with:

5. Purification of the heart, 4:8. James enjoins his readers to "purify your hearts." These statements say it all. "The hand speaks of one's outward actions and the heart depicts his inward thoughts. The first toward God, and the only one that will bring God nigh unto us, is the consciousness and confession of inner depravity" (Strauss). (For the meaning of "double-minded" please see my comments on James 1:18). Dear friend, I believe in having a periodic confession session with my God. "If we confess our sins, He is faithful and righteous to forgive us our sins and to cleanse us from all unrighteousnes" (I John 1:9). To "confess" is a compound word in the Greek, from two words: (1) "same" and (2) "to say." The word "confess" means "to say the same thing as" or "to agree with." When one confesses his sins, in essence he is agreeing with God that they must go! Not *just* the naming of the sins, as in a Roman Catholic confessional; but, a literal abandoning of them as well. Proverbs puts it this way: "...But he who confesses and forsakes them will find compassion" (28:13). This brings us to:

6. Miserableness, 4:9. Verse 9 says, "Be miserable." This doesn't convey the thought that first pops into our heads at the first reading. The legalist won't agree because he has sold us a bill of goods that if we enjoy something, we are in sin. The legalistic test for spirituality is how miserable you are. According to the legalist, if you are miserable, you must be spiritual. That is why the average Christian isn't *enjoying* the Christian life, he is *enduring* it. That is not what "miserable" means in verse 9. This is the natural result of a productive confession session. When one has "locked horns" with the realities of sin, he must feel like a lethal wretch. Sin killed Christ. It wasn't the nails that held Him to the cross; it was *our sin*. That makes me miserable enough to change! This brings us to:

7. Mourning, 4:9. The misery of sin should cause one to "mourn." This is a sorrow deeper than even the sorrow of weeping. It is godly sorrow. Paul writes of it, "For the sorrow that is according to the will of God produces a repentance without regret, leading to salvation; but the sorrow of the world produces death" (II Cor. 7:10). This is more than mere "crocodile tears." Rather it is the wrenching of one's heart in chronic remorse which does manifest itself in:

8. Weeping, 4:9. James says, "Weep." This is the external result of inner sorrow. The word that James uses expresses hurt to the point of wailing. Yes, sin brings pain and pain brings weeping. But, someday Christ "shall wipe away every tear from their eyes; and there shall no longer be any death; there shall no longer be any mourning, or crying, or pain..." (Rev. 21:4). Notice that the word "tear" is singular. Which means that the Lord Jesus will wipe away every, single, individual tear. He will be the personal minister of us all!

Verse 9 also says, "Let your laughter be turned into mourning, and your joy to gloom." Simply stated, what makes us glad and sad tells much about us. The need is:

9. Humility before the Lord, 4:10. "Humble yourselves" is reflexive and means to allow yourselves to be humbled. God will humble us if we permit it. God's way of greatness is down (Phil. 2:5-11). This is the opposite of the world's way of self-assertiveness and competitiveness.

Correspondingly, "He will exalt you." This is the Christian's success story. Please see my comment on James 4:7. The tenth commandment is that of:

10. Speaking no evil, 4:11. James, in his characteristic style, has much to say about the tongue. In verse 11 he again mentions abusive speech. "Do not speak against one another, brethren...." God, through James, is solidly rebuking these brethren for practicing destructive criticism of one another. God calls this "backbiting." Simply defined, it is the function of biting someone's head off behind his back. The contemporary concept is "slander" and the Bible forbids it (Ps. 15:3; Prov. 25:23; Rom. 1:30; II Cor. 12:20). Lord, set a sentinel on my speech!

9

The Life
with No Lord

THE CHAPTER OUTLINED:

113

I. INNUENDOES ABOUT OTHERS IS SIN, 4:11

James is at it once again; namely the tongue. And, I believe, rightfully so. I believe that sins of the tongue are in the grossest sin area that exist. It is high time that the tide of the tongue is stemmed. Much salvaging needs to be done to recover the torrential spoils that the tongue has caused! The tongue is like a toothache; the longer it is neglected, the worse it becomes!

Verse 11 is not mentioning appreciative accolades. It is incredulous how some Christians can abuse with an infectious verbosity. What's more; whereas the church is to be a whole new look for the world, it has literally "turned off" many searching souls with the mobility of the mouths of some of its members! These "mouth-manipulators" are generally so "holier-than-thou" that if it were possible for a vacancy to ever occur in the Trinity, they would be the first to apply. Yet, with their deranged discourse, they verbally destroy others! God save the mouth!

James is pointed: "He who speaks against a brother, or judges his brother, speaks against the law, and judges the law...."

"Speaks against" is literally "one who talks down" someone else. It is the self-appointed critic (Matt. 7:1). To judge is a function that only God can undertake (Rom. 14). These Jews understood the law and who gave it. By censuring one another by means of destructive and disruptive criticism, they were assuming God-like functions. They were doing what God alone can do.

All of us, who love the Lord, should be servants of the Lord and brothers one to another. When we judge the motives of someone else's heart, we simply demonstrate that we lack humility. As a rule of thumb one usually runs down another in order to build himself up.

An important reason to refrain from belittling another is that by criticizing or judging, one assumes the right to judge the law. This would be absolutely abhorring to a Jew. He would be judging the law by disobeying the law. His action toward the law would indicate that he considered it a bad law or one which was unworthy of his obedience. By doing this he would be assuming the position of the Lawgiver. This is blasphemous since there is only one Lawgiver, and that is God. Matthew 10:28 makes this perfectly clear! As Moses wrote, "See now that I, I am He, and there is no god besides Me; It is I who put to death and give life..." (Deut. 32:39). Therefore, if you gossip, criticize, or judge someone else, you are usurping God's position! Be very careful! "Therefore you are without excuse, every man of you who passes judgment, for in that you judge another, you condemn yourself; for you who judge practice the same things" (Rom. 2:1).

II. THE INIQUITY OF JUDGING OTHERS, 4:12

Verse 12 simply repeats more of the same from verse 11. It is, nevertheless, those things about the tongue which bear repeating. God is the one and *only* Lawgiver as well as the one and *only* Judge. Paul adds,

> ...but the one who examines me is the Lord. Therefore do not go on passing judgment before the time, but wait until the Lord comes who will both bring to light the things hidden in the darkness and disclose the motives of men's hearts... (I Cor. 4:4-5).

God is omniscient; therefore, God is Judge. I Kings 8:39, "...Thou alone dost know the hearts of all the sons of men." I Chronicles 28:9, "...for the Lord searches all hearts, and understands every intent of the thoughts...." Yes, God is the *only* Judge, for He alone knows the heart of man (I Sam. 16:7; Job 10:4; Prov. 15:11).

God is the only one who is superior to His own Law. The one who judges seizes God's sole prerogative as the source of life and death. Competing with God is skating on thin ice or walking on eggs!

III. INDEPENDENCE IS SIN, 4:13

Atheism is a weird thing. It is the ignominious denial of the existence of God. The word is from the Greek *theos* (God) and *a* (a letter of negation hence; "no God"). The atheist (the fool) is weird because according to the Scriptures he says, "There is no God..." (Ps. 14:1).

The other day I was sharing the good news of salvation in Christ with a man who professed to be an atheist. His ultimate goal in life is to *prove* that there is no God. I sensed something strange, alien and even unnerving about this ambition. I thought—if there is no God, then why does one have to prove it? I asked the man: "Why are you trying to prove that there is no God?" He replied, "To rid the world of the God-delusion!" I retorted, "I don't believe that at all! No one has to prove there is no God, if there is no God; unless, of course, he has an axe to grind!" The ensuing silence seemed endless and was almost deafening. That serves to illustrate that atheism is nothing more than a convenient removal from a life that with which one has to eventually deal. There is a tendency in us all to avoid the unpleasant. The tendency in many is to regard God as a disturbing factor since He will, indeed, alter the life! In order not to reckon with Him, then why not just banish Him from the heart and legislate Him out of the classroom?

Obviously, a Christian cannot relate to atheistic mentality. But, would you believe that a Christian can become a *practical* atheist? He may act independent of the Lord and that, my friend, is *sin*!

The overall context of chapter 4 has been the replacing of a world-centered viewpoint with a submission to God. In verse 13, we are introduced to the unsubmissive Christian business man, who acts independently of a sovereign God. He plans his enterprises in his own self-sufficiency totally omitting the will of God in his exchanges and schemes.

James writes, "Come now." Our contemporary culture would say it like this: "Do you really think you can make your own plans and determine your own fate?"

James continues, "You who say." The plural form of this statement indicates that there are many who disregard the providence of God. It is God who permits the profits in the business world; it is not the ingenuity of the business man! "...And what do you have that you did not receive? But if you did receive it, why do you boast as if you had not received it" (I Cor. 4:7). The scholar's scholar, Spiros Zodiates illustrates:

> Planning without God, whether we execute our plans or not, will bring us nothing but misery. Robert Horton has well said that the greatest lesson he learned from life was that people who set their minds and hearts on money are equally disappointed whether they get it or not. It binds alike the poor who crave money and the rich who make it their god. Let us, therefore, ask God's partnership in all that we plan for our lives, if we want our lives to count, not only for time and men, but also for eternity and God.

How did these "*practical* atheists" plan? They postulated: "Today or tomorrow, we shall go to such and such a city, and spend a year there and engage in business and make a profit." Remember that these were Jewish Christians of the *diaspora* and many of them were shrewd, both in their methods and in their contacts, among the business community. It seems as if Jews everywhere make accomplished business persons. But James questions their wisdom when God is left out of their dealings.

"Engage in business" is a most practical term, which describes a commonplace occurrence in the game of life. Coming from the Greek root *emporeuomai* is the English "emporium," which is a place of trade or a commercial center. Certainly, no one who loves America, will question the validity of the free-enterprise system. It has done much to strengthen our country. But, if God is arbitrarily banished from the system, then it is absolutely valueless.

In their own self-confidence, and in their reliance upon their products (which evidently sold themselves because they were so good), these Jewish merchants would plan a business trip "...and spend a year there..." They did so in order to "make a profit." My fellow believers, there is nothing wrong with making a profit! That is what business is all about. But to do so, without trusting in the divine sovereignty of Almighty God is folly of the worst sort. Dr. Spiros Zodiates again assists:

> Profit-making had become a passion with these merchants. That was the only reason why they traveled, why they traded, why they lived... Oh, vain man, who with one hand holds the present and with the other the future, you don't stop to realize that it is only by the sustaining grace of God that you own this very instant in which you live! These merchants did not look far enough. We must look into the future in terms of eternity and not only in terms of tomorrow's gain. Their aspirations were high, but they were not high enough. They stacked up profits, but not heavenly treasures while here on earth.

Acting independently of the Lord is living like an atheist. To do your own thing, in the Christian life, is totally out of place. The calamity of this concept is even further compounded when one considers:

IV. THE IRONY OF THE SHORTNESS OF LIFE, 4:14

One of the most awesome statements of Scripture is recorded in verse 14 of James chapter 4: "Yet you do not know what your life will be like tomorrow." The key word is "know." The Greek word conveys the idea of knowing for sure, being absolutely certain. James is saying there are *no* guarantees in this life apart from the Lord and His will and Word.

How true this is. In the course of one month, I was personally involved in these things: I performed a funeral for a stillborn baby. Next, I officiated at the funeral of a three-month-old infant who died in his crib. Later that day, my telephone rang in my study, and the party on the other end asked me to pray for a fifteen-year-old boy who had total kidney failure. He was surviving due to a dialysis machine. Just last week, I conducted the funeral of a man who left a seventeen year old widow behind. He was twenty-two. We expect the old to die, but not the young. Somehow we think that the young are guaranteed a long life.

How possible is it for man to know his own universe? About as possible for him to *know* for sure that he will live to see tomorrow's sunrise. It will take man four light years to go to the nearest star from planet earth. And, this is traveling at 186,000 miles per second. That is what James is stating in the first half of verse 14: "Yet you do not know what your life will be like tomorrow...."

The *only* thing I am sure of is that I am saved and that the Bible is the Word of God. I wonder how many times I have been swimming in the ocean. I have been down deep with a scuba tank on several occasions. Why haven't I been assaulted by a rogue shark, who, in his tiny brain, set up territorial rights where I happened to be swimming? Paul says it like this: "But by the grace of God I am what I am..." (I Cor. 15:10). I live this moment by His grace. My blood circulates because of Him. I am going to heaven by His grace (Eph. 2:8-9).

Life is uncertain. Do not take it for granted! From the Wisdom Literature we read: "Do not boast about tomorrow, for you do not know what a day may bring forth" (Prov. 27:1).

The last half of verse 14 speaks of the brevity of life. It tersely says, "You are just a vapor that appears for a little while and then vanishes away." Job reads: "My days are swifter than a weaver's shuttle, and come to an end without hope" (Job 7:6). David says in part: "...Let me know how transient I am. Behold, Thou hast made my days as handbreadths, and my lifetime as nothing in Thy sight, surely every man at his best is a mere breath" (Ps. 39:4-5). David reiterates later: "Man is like the mere breath; his days are like a passing shadow" (Ps. 144:4).

James compares one's life to a "vapor." What is man? A puff of smoke, air, mist—one minute he is there, the next he is not.

Remember what David said in Psalm 39:4-7 (quoted in part above). It is a great discovery to learn what we are in comparison to God and His Person. Our lives are like soap bubbles and they may pop at any moment! Read about the rich fool in Luke 12:16-21. His life style was the same as contemporary society's: "...And I said to my soul, 'Soul, you have many goods laid up for many years to come; take your ease, eat, drink and be merry'..." (12:19). He thought that life went on and on like the sun sets and rises. He thought that *things* would make him happy. Well, he died in the middle of the night and he couldn't take *one* of the things to hell with him—not *one*! It is as Matthew says, "For what will a man be profited, if he gains the whole world, and forfeits his soul? Or what will a man give in exchange for his soul?" (Matt. 16:26).

This is most meaningful, as we need to make the most of what we have, while we still have the time, for the glory of God (I Cor. 3:13-15). So, my friend, "redeem the time." Paul warns, "Making the most of your time, because the days are evil" (Eph. 5:16). May our prayer be that of David's: "So teach us to number our days, that we may present to Thee a heart of wisdom" (Ps. 90:12). This is why:

V. INDIFFERENCE TO GOD IS SIN, 4:15

James commences verse 15 with the word "Instead." The grammatical intention is "instead of your saying," which refers back to the *practical* atheists of verse 13 and his plans minus God. Rather than business calculations, without considering God, "you ought to say": is the proper viewpoint being pressed here?

This view is, "If the Lord wills, we shall live and also do this or that." The statement "if the Lord wills" is a third class condition. In other words, maybe God will will it, or maybe He will not; but, let us assume for the sake of argument, at this point, that He does will it. Therefore, a business man or anyone else for that matter, should make all of his plans subject to change upon "Divine Notice." The general attitude of "If God wills" is to be always in the heart. Proverbs again sheds light: "Trust in the Lord with all your heart, and do not lean on your own understanding. In all your ways acknowledge Him, and He will make your paths straight" (Prov. 3:5-6). A. T. Robertson adds that this is "the proper attitude of mind (Acts 18:21; I Cor. 4:19; 16:7; Rom. 1:19; Phil. 2:19, 24; Heb. 6:3)."

Indifference to God and His will is sin. To disregard the Lord results in dire consequences. Recall the incident in Joshua 9:14, "So the men of Israel took some of their provisions, and did not ask for the counsel of the Lord." Therefore they were deceived by the Gibeonites and disobeyed the Lord. God was not consulted, so His mind was not known on the subject, and ill-boding results were introduced. There was a covenant made with Gibeon. Three days later, the plot was exposed. In the practical words of Dr. J. Sidlow Baxter, "We need not only the *power* of the Spirit against giants, but the *wisdom* of the Spirit against serpents!" Satan is far easier to strike down as a son of Anak in warrior's armor than as a disguised Gibeonite in some pity-voking beggar's attire. Satan's subtle wiles are more dangerous than his open assaults. He is more dangerous as "an angel of light" than as "a roaring lion." The league with these Canaanites held evil possibilities. It imperiled Israel's faith. It was not made because of any breakdown of Israel's faith at that time, but faith had been thrown off guard. Here in this ninth chapter (of Joshua) *faith is endangered* by the failure to refer everything to God.

A believer *must* acknowledge his utter dependence upon the Lord whenever a business deal, scheme or plan of any sort is enacted. What is more "everyday" than committing every area of that day to God. A copious amount of faith is mandatory for a meaningful life; and that faith must be proliferous.

The correct and practical approach to life and its multifaceted complexities is simply to acknowledge: "If the Lord wills, we shall live and also do this or that." If we lived in the good of this verse we could live life to the fullest and worry not at all. But, when one makes ironclad plans, without God, then he is prone to worry since his planning is homocentric rather than theocentric. James encompasses the entire gamut of life: time, travel, talents. treasure, length of stay, activity and the like. God is to be integral in the part and parcel of *all* one does! It is not wrong to plan, *if* it is God's will and *if* it is subject to change with God's will. This attitude adds to all the amenities of all of one's activities!

If one is laboring for the glory of God (I Cor. 10:31), he will consult the will of God in all matters. This will greatly affect even his business routines. As Jesus says it: "Do not work for the food which perishes, but for the food which endures to eternal life, which the Son of Man shall give to you, for on Him the Father, even God, has set His seal" (John 6:27). When this mentality pervades every pattern of one's life then this jubilant acclamation will be produced: "The Lord has done great things for us; we are glad" (Ps. 126:3). Prepare perceptively and God will grant the blessings and the victories, and the needs.

VI. INSENSITIVENESS TO GOD IS SIN, 4:16

These Jewish Christians were not giving credit to whom credit was due. As a matter of fact, some had become quite insensitive to their source of wealth, help and strength; namely, God. Verse 16 begins: "But as it is." The word "but" is a strong word of contrast. In contrast to the way it should be, "it is" shows that "now" pride had magnified the big "I" in place of God's grace. God makes a man the way he is! But when man begins to assert the colossal "I," he is in big trouble with a mighty big God. An ant has never defied me; in like manner, may I never defy God!

How tragic to read: "...you boast in your arrogance...." He is a braggart and a boaster and his arrogance is forever on his lips. How different this is to the humility of life that James has been discussing (4:6, 10). The opposite of humility is arrogance or presumption. But, when this superior-type of person fails or has rough waters he blames God.

This was the situation in Numbers 12. It was absolute insensitiveness to God. The "mixed multitude" or the "tares" were at it again! They were insensitive to the things of God and cold to His will. In chapter 12 the murmuring of these negative people had been so potent that it had turned the very brother and sister of Moses against him. They were contentiously questioning even his right to lead. Well, God lowered the boom on these critics of His chosen one. Miriam, the instigator, was stricken with leprosy. It is a serious sin to speak against God's leadership! Obviously, Moses was vindicated (Num. 12:4-10).

In chapter 13, Moses dispatched a survey crew to appraise the land of Canaan. For forty days the land was spied. They returned with a glowing report (13:27). As long as their focal point was upon God and His leadership, all was positive. But, as soon as they said "Nevertheless" (13:28), their perspective became negative. This is the big "but" of the Bible! Ten of the spies were the "mixed multitude" or the "tares." They were the pour-cold-water-on-it parties who seem to penetrate every congregation. You can usually identify them by the seven last words of the church: "We've never done it that way before!"

Then Joshua and Caleb, who had the "Divine Viewpoint," said: "...We should by all means go up and take possession of it, for we shall surely overcome it" (13:30). The negative people seemed to be winning, for their illogical logic is recorded in Numbers 13:31-33. The fruit of the negative people is seen in Numbers 14:1, "Then all the congregation lifted up their voice and cried, and the people wept that night." The tares seemed to be on top because they influenced the people to stone the leadership (14:2-10). These negative oriented, ornery people talked themselves, and anyone else who would listen, into a nervous breakdown.

My dear friend, this is one of the most tragic accounts in all of the Word of God! You either will be a *murmurer* or a *missionary*; but, you *are* not and cannot be both!

Have you ever heard of a church dying? Well, I have, many times. There is only *one* reason for the death of a church and that is disobedience. When a man becomes arrogant and disobeys God and turns against the leadership of the church, that church dies. The choice is simple: obey God and be *blessed*; disobey and be *blighted*!

Arrogance is no more than an attitude of insensitiveness to God and God's leaders. It is expressing your opinion above His Word. It is disobedience to Him and His representatives! James calls a spade a spade: "...all such boasting is evil." In the same boat with this is that:

VII. INDECISION IS SIN, 4:17

Pointedly written: "Therefore, to one who knows the right thing to do, and does not do it, to him it is sin." "To one who knows" immediately informs the reader that the person in question knows what James has in mind. These Christian business men *know* that humility, dependence upon the Lord, and a theocentric life style are indispensable to the Christian life. This speaks of sins of omission. It is a Biblical truism that increased knowledge brings increased responsibility. Jesus reemphasizes, "And that slave who knew his master's will and did not get ready or act in accord with his will, shall receive many lashes, but the one who did not know it, and committed deeds worthy of a flogging, will receive but few. And from everyone who has been given much shall much be required; and to whom they entrusted much, of him they will ask all the more" (Luke 12:47-48).

The phrase "the right thing to do" means that they knew that independent activity without God was sin. These are sins of omission as defined by Christ: "Woe to you, scribes and Pharisees, hypocrites! For you tithe mint and dill and cummin, and have neglected the weightier provisions of the law: justice and mercy and faithfulness; but these are the things you should have done without neglecting the others" (Matt. 23:23). There was a gap between their "Spiritual I.Q.'s" and their "Spiritual I Do's."

This is a great parallel to Jonah. Jonah *knew* that God had called him to be the first foreign missionary. God told Jonah to go to Nineveh. But Jonah knew that Ninevah was one of the most wicked cities on the face of the earth. Jonah was afraid to go there, and who can blame him? Baxter quotes from John Urquhart about the Assyrians:

> Without a doubt, the Assyrians were the German Nazis of those days. The inscriptions on Assyrian monuments which have been interpreted for us by our archaeologists reveal how they revelled in hideous cruelty on those whom they vanquished.
>
> ...Some of the victims were held down while one of the band of torturers, who are portrayed upon the monuments gloating fiendishly over their fearful work, inserts his hand into the victim's mouth, grips his tongue and wrenches it out by the roots. In another spot pegs are driven into the ground. To these, another victim's wrists are fixed with cords. His ankles are similarly made fast, and the man is stretched out, unable to move a muscle. The exectioner than applies himself to his task; and beginning at the accustomed spot, the sharp knife makes its incision, the skin is raised inch by inch till the man is flayed alive. These skins are then stretched out upon the city walls, or otherwise disposed of so as to terrify the people and leave behind long enduring impressions of Assyrian vengeance. For others, long sharp poles are prepared. The sufferer, taken like all the rest from the leading men of the city, is laid down; the sharpened end of the pole is driven in through the lower part of the chest; the pole is then raised, bearing the writhing victim aloft; it is planted in the hole dug for it, and the man is left to die.

...Pyramids of human heads marked the path of the conqueror; boys and girls were burnt alive or reserved for a worse fate; men were impaled, flayed alive, blinded or deprived of their hands and feet, of their ears and noses, while the women and children were carried into slavery, the captured city plundered and reduced to ashes...

I am most positive that every Israeli knew about Nineveh and all of the loathsome and savagely brutal atrocities which were commonplace there. If I were in Jonah's situation, I would convulsively shake with fear if God said: "Roy, go to Nineveh and preach!" I would respond about eight octaves higher: "Who, me?" Nahum had often spoken of the evils of Assyria:

The oracle of Nineveh. The book of the vision of Nahum the Elkoshite. A jealous and avenging God is the Lord; the Lord is avenging and wrathful. The Lord takes vengeance on His adversaries, and He reserves wrath for His enemies...The lion [Nineveh] tore enough for his cubs, killed enough for his lionesses, and filled his lairs with prey and his dens with torn flesh...Woe to the bloody city, completely full of lies and pillage; her prey never departs. The noise of the whip, the noise of the rattling of the wheel, galloping horses, and bounding chariots! Horsemen charging, swords flashing, spears gleaming, many slain, a mass or corpses, and countless dead bodies—They stumble over the dead bodies! All because of the many harlotries of the harlot, the charming one, the mistress of sorceries, who sells nations by her harlotries and families by her sorceries... There is no relief for your breakdown, your wound is incurable. All who hear about you [the report of impending doom] will clap their hands over you, for on whom has not your evil passed continually? (Nahum 1:1-2; 2:2-12; 3:1-4; 3:19).

But, James means what He says and says what he means: "...to one who knows the right thing to do, and does it not, to him it is sin" (James 4:17). God instructed Jonah to go and he was indecisive and thereby sinned. To make a long story short, Jonah was thrown off a ship as he was sailing in the opposite direction *away from* Ninevah! A great fish, especially prepared by God for Jonah, swallowed him. To be in that fish's belly (yuk!) or to be in Nineveh preaching was the option. He re-covenanted with God, and that fish *vomited* out Jonah on the shore and he *ran* to and through Nineveh. Jonah would rather obey God than be digested alive by a fish on any day of the week!

Well, what happened in Nineveh is a matter of record (Jonah 3). The entire, wicked city repented! It was some kind of city. Just the distance around it was sixty miles or a three days journey (Jonah 3:3). This means that Nineveh was three hundred and fifty square miles. It has been estimated that its population was about one million people and probably more. This is a powerful narrative. When God lays out what is right, we had rather be dead than disobey! If you doubt that a million people repented, then listen to this: "Then the people of Nineveh believed in God; and they called a fast and put on sackcloth from the greatest to the least of them. When the word reached the King of Ninevah, he arose from his throne, laid aside his robe from him, covered himself with sackcloth, and sat on the ashes" (Jonah 3:5-6). Still have doubts? The words of Jesus are the clincher: "...This generation is a wicked generation; it seeks for a sign, and yet no sign shall be given to it but the sign of Jonah. For just as Jonah became a sign to the Ninevites, so shall the Son of Man be to this generation" (Luke 11:29-30).

Dear ones, the Word of God tells us what we are to do. All of us have been warned just like Joshua and Caleb warned the Israelis and Jonah warned the Ninevites. The facts have been laid out in front of us. To persist in the idiocy of the arrogant and self-confident manner of living is folly. The future is uncertain and it is out of our hands and in the hands of God. You're in good hands with the Almighty. Friends, I may not know what the future holds; but, I do know Him who holds the future! Do you?

Mother, Where's the Money?

THE CHAPTER OUTLINED:

I. Concerning **SORROW**, 5:1

II. Concerning **SECURITY**, 5:2-3
   A. Riches, 5:2
   B. Garments, 5:2
   C. Gold and Silver, 5:3

III. Concerning **SELFISHNESS**, 5:4-6
   A. **CHEATING** 5:4
   B. **COMFORT**, 5:5
   C. **CONDEMNING** the Righteous, 5:6

There are three Divine warnings to the rich:

I. CONCERNING SORROW, 5:1

James snaps the reader to attention when he writes: "Come now, you rich...." *Plutocrat* comes from the root form of this word *ploutos*. Obviously, he is addressing himself to the rich. But, he is doing this for the benefit of his believing readers. Mitton perceptively states: "Their intention is not to awaken the rich to a sense of their imminent peril, but rather to dissuade hesitant Christians from falling into a foolish attitude of envy towards the powers and privileges which wealth seems to confer on those who possess it." Believers are being equipped with a proper perspective toward riches. He is writing to "brethren" (v. 7). As Rosscup observes:

> By faith, they are to take God's long-range viewpoint of life and be assured of judgment upon the unjust. It is true that wealthy men who harm them now have the upper hand and appear to be immovably established. But their reckoning with the Lord must inevitably come. Thus faith invests one with patience to endure rather than succumb. The "rich" are unsaved men, as in 2:2-6, and not saved as is possible for the rich brother in 1:10 who is humbled by faith's scale of values toward God's gift and things.

The "rich" are to be understood as unsaved for the following reasons:

1. There is a clear-cut distinction between the type of rich men in view here and the "righteous" (5:6).

2. The parallel between the rich in 2:2-6 and here is so obvious that James must have the same group in mind both times.

CHAPTER TWO	CHAPTER FIVE
V. 6—the rich oppress the believers and personally drag them into court.	V. 6—the rich condemn and put to death the believers.

3. The Old Testament prophets are often scathing in their denunciation of the rich who oppress the poor (Amos 2:6-8; Hab. 2:9). James is Jewish and most familiar with these things; therefore, he is evidently denouncing, in a similar way, the rich who persecute the poor.

4. Christ Himself often referred to the rich in this manner and He definitely meant the unsaved rich (Matt. 23:13-36; Mark 12:15; Luke 18:24-25).

It is important to note that riches per se are amoral. The morality comes into play with what one does with them. In this first verse of James chapter 5, it is clear that if the rich do not entertain tears of repentance now, there will be tears of anguish later. The unsaved rich are to "weep and howl." These are two of the strongest words depicting outbursts of the deepest sort from a grief-stricken heart. These "miseries" are just around the corner (James 4:14). "Which are coming upon you." This reveals the *certainty* and *inevitability* of this sentence of condemnation (James 5:7). Here comes the Judge and He is standing at the door!

There is no question about it, trusting in riches brings sorrow in the here and now and in the hereafter. When a man trusts in things, and things are taken away, misery results. Wealth hinders people from becoming Christians. They trust in their *pocketbooks* and not in the *Person* of Christ (Mark 10:23-27). Sometimes wealth hinders even the Christian from the victorious life (I Tim. 6:17). Indeed, riches give a false sense of values (Luke 12:15). Riches also give a false sense of security (Luke 12:16-21).

The words of wisdom in I Timothy 6:10 are still in the Bible: "For the love of money is a root of all sorts of evil, and some by longing for it have wandered away from the faith, and pierced themselves with a pang." The wisest man who ever lived, who also had much wealth, said: "There is a grievous evil which I have seen under the sun: riches being hoarded by their owner to his hurt" (Eccles. 5:13). Money can captivate a man's heart and thereby control him! Money breaks and divides homes and ruins lives! Let us ever be reminded that riches, not properly used under the hand of God, cause sorrow. The second thing that James says about money in chapter 5 is:

II. CONCERNING SECURITY, 5:2-3

Security is like an elusive dream. Everybody seeks it; but, no one has it really! Commercials advertising the security of savings and loan institutions are telling us that our deposits are now insured up to $40,000 by an agency of the Federal Goverment. We are told by an expert to have six months' earnings in a savings account. One organization reassures us with "Know that you've put your money in exactly the right place." Somehow money is supposed to give us security. However, James is saying in verses 2 and 3 that just the opposite is the case. Money *lacks* security. Riches are *temporal* and *tarnishable*. James selects three categories, in which some rich people amassed things, in his generation, which represent the fact that all such things do pass away:

A. RICHES, 5:2. James writes, "Your riches have rotted." These riches are represented in food and supplies which the ancients prized so highly

(Luke 12:18). "Have rotted" is the perfect tense which generally denotes past action with results that continue into the present. As Robertson comments, "The perfect tense presents the state of rottenness. This ill-gotten gain will not keep; it is always putrid. There is such a thing as tainted money—blood money wrung from the oppressed toilers...." The second area of wealth which James discusses is:

B. GARMENTS, 5:2. Much is meant by: "...your garments have become moth-eaten." "Garments" means outer garments like our modern suits or coats. The finer the clothing, the more successful was the ancient entrepreneur in the estimation of his colleagues. But, the mighty moth attacked these pieces of finery 2,000 years ago, just like he does now. This is again reinforced by the use of the perfect tense of the verb.

C. GOLD and SILVER, 5:3. James says that their gold and silver "have rusted." For the third time, the perfect is the tense of the verb demonstrating that even today precious metals rust. But, alas, the critic takes a potshot at the Bible and says herein lies an error—gold and silver do not rust. The answer is that even those of New Testament times were intelligent enough to realize that everything on this earth, including gold and silver is in the process of *decay*. John has noted so clearly: "And the world is passing away..." (I John 2:17). John employs the present tense, thus revealing that the habitual characteristic of this world is decay, rust and decomposition. In the words of Donald Burdick:

> The present tense indicates that it is even now in the process of dissolution. By its very nature evil is self-destructive. The world system of evil carries within itself forces which are causing its own deterioration; and ultimately when Christ returns to establish His Kingdom, He will completely destroy it.

Hoarded wealth "and their rust will be a witness against you and will consume your flesh like fire." How sobering are these words! If a man trusts in riches rather than in Christ, he will burn in hell (Matt. 25:41). "It is in the Last Days that you have stored up your treasure!" This is a phrase denoting the whole elastic period of messianic times. The rich were doing this very thing even in the time of Messiah! They are doing it now and will continue to do it to the very moment of Messiah's second advent. Those very riches in which men have sought security will be as rust when it witnesses against them. It will consume the "flesh" rapidly. These words should decimate any misdirected confidences that we might have in riches, for they are uncertain and they will judge us.

Listen to the voice of one of the greatest of ancient monarchs:

I enlarged my works: I built houses for myself, I planted vineyards for myself; I made gardens and parks for myself, and I planted in them all kinds of fruit trees; I made ponds of water for myself from which to irrigate a forest of growing trees. I bought male and female slaves, and I had homeborn slaves. Also I possessed flocks and herds larger than all who preceded me in Jerusalem. Also, I collected for myself silver and gold, and the treasure of kings and provinces. I provided for myself male and female singers and the pleasures of men—many concubines. Then I became great and increased more than all who preceded me in Jerusalem. My wisdom also stood by me. And all that my eyes desired I did not refuse them. I did not withhold my heart from any pleasure, for my heart was pleased because of all my labor and this was my reward for all my labor. Thus I considered all my activities which my hands had done and the labor which I had exerted, and behold all was vanity and striving after wind and there was no profit under the sun (Eccles. 2:4-11).

But, where is true value to be found? The Lord is our true value. Psalm 73:25 eloquently adds: "Whom have I in heaven but Thee? And besides Thee, I desire nothing on earth." Where is there true security? The Lord is our true security. Again the Psalms contribute: "The Lord is my shepherd, I shall not want" (23:1). The Lord is the only investment with a guaranteed eternal return. Moses exclaims, "The eternal God is a dwelling place, and underneath are the everlasting arms" (Deut. 33:27).

Oh, my dear friend, this is where our emphases are to be always placed! The Biblical emphasis of life is not temporal, but eternal. The Biblical emphasis of life is not material, but spiritual. Money may make the *mare* run; but, the love of it will damn the *man!*

"I have coveted no one's silver or gold or clothes" (Acts 20:33). Riches deceive and Paul knew that he was to be rich toward God (Luke 12:21). Money can only have eternal value as it is used for God's will and glory. The inner man is an imperishable thing in this world (II Cor. 4:16). Therefore our number one priority is to give glory to the Lord Jesus Christ (I Cor. 10:31). Now:

III. CONCERNING SELFISHNESS, 5:4-6

This is viewed in three ways; the first is:

A. CHEATING, 5:4. The problem of the love of money had caused these rich people to deal unjustly with their hired labor force. This was a matter of moral obligation and by withholding what was owed was nothing more than stealing and cheating.

"Behold" has been referred to by some as the "stop, look and listen" sign of the Bible. Whenever this word occurs, we are to sit up and take notice for important truth is forthcoming.

"The pay" means "wages" and is translated that way in Matthew 20:8. These wages were being unpaid to "the laborers who mowed your fields." "Laborers" is from the Greek word from which the English derives its term "energy." It shows diligence and industriousness.

The defrauding of part of the laborers' proper wages "cries out against you." This is the collective cry of the workers for rightful recompense which was theirs. A. T. Robertson observes: "Pitiful picture of earned wages kept back by rich Jews, old problem of capital and labour that is with us yet in acute form." Today we have unions and management who undergo arbitration processes. The working man of our day is greatly protected in comparison to these first century laborers; but, unfortunately, he is still "ripped off" by the rich in some cases. However, the status and the situation of our laboring people are far better than their ancient counterparts. In those days, there were no unions, strikes, walk-outs, sit-downs, hitting the bricks, arbitration, settlements, contracts, benefits and retirement programs. Exploitation was the name of the game.

Even though there was no place for the maltreated worker to appeal, "the outcry of those who did the harvesting has reached the ears of the Lord of Sabaoth." This is a term that depicts God in His omnipotence (Isa. 1:9; Rom. 9:29). When God, who is the *only* all-powerful one, takes sides against someone else, look out in all directions!

The type of injustice in verse 5 is frequently condemned in the Old Testament (Lev. 19:13; Prov. 3:27-28; Jer. 22:13; Amos 8:4; Mal. 3:5). Moses expresses the intent well:

> You shall not oppress a hired servant who is poor and needy, whether he is one of your countrymen or one of your aliens who is in your land in your towns. You shall give him his wages on his day before the sun sets, for he is poor and sets his heart on it; so that he may not cry against you to the Lord and it become sin in you (Deut. 24:14-15).

In the light of Mosaic law, what the rich were doing was very, very bad. You see, payday was everyday for all the people. The reason why the wages and the poor cried out was because the daily work provided the daily living and the rich were withholding their very livelihood. But the rich land barons are reminded that the Sovereign God is the All-powerful Champion in vindicating wrongs. He will defeat all the wicked rich and put down all oppression. Who needs *communism* when you've got *Christ!* Who needs *socialism* when you have the *Saviour!*

There are some important principles here for you and me who live in the twentieth century. Romans 13:8 succinctly states, "Owe nothing to anyone except to love one another...." We are to pay our bills on time and strive for the goal of being debt free.

Allow me to give one more application. Ephesians 6:7-9 records:

> With good will render service, as to the Lord, and not to men, knowing that whatever good thing each one does, this he will receive back from the Lord, whether slave or free. And, masters, do the same things to them, and give up threatening, knowing that both their Master and yours is in heaven, and there is no partiality with Him.

This is sound advice for both employer and employee alike. In essence, both of you are to know that God does right by you, so you do right by each other. The second manifestation of selfishness of the unsaved rich is:

B. COMFORT, 5:5. The ancient, poor laborers were diseased, exploited and their lives were hanging by thin threads. Contrasted to them were the overindulgent wealthy, who were living in their luxury and plush comfort. The crime of comfort is viewed from the perspective that the rich lived at the expense of the poor. In the words of James: "You have lived luxuriously on the earth and led a life of wanton pleasure; you have fattened your hearts in a day of slaughter" (5:5).

"You have lived luxuriously" speaks of the softness and ease of their existence. This luxurious living is depicted in Luke 7:25, "But what did you go out to see? A man dressed in soft clothing? Behold, those who are splendidly clothed and live in luxury are found in royal palaces." Oh, the wisdom of the qualifying phrase: "...on the earth..." for that is the only place where the ungodly rich will experience softness! Listen and learn from the rich man of Luke 16:19-25:

> Now there was a certain rich man, and he habitually dressed in purple and fine linen, gaily living in splendor every day. And a certain poor man named Lazarus was laid at his gate, covered with sores. Now it came about that the poor man died and he was carried away by the angels to Abraham's bosom; and the rich man also died and was buried. And in Hades he lifted up his eyes, being in torment, and saw Abraham far away, and Lazarus in his bosom. And he cried out and said, "Father Abraham, have mercy on me, and send Lazarus, that he may dip the tip of his finger in water and cool off my tongue; for I am in agony in this flame." But Abraham said, "Child, remember that during your life you received your good things, and likewise Lazarus bad things; but now he is being comforted here, and you are in agony."

James continues in verse 5, reminding the unsaved rich that on the earth they "*led a life of wanton pleasure*." The idea is that of voluptuousness and riotousness. We are reminded of the lewd woman of I Timothy 5:6, "But she who gives herself to wanton pleasure is dead even while she lives." It is hard to believe that such injustices and inequities have existed and do exist. Commenting, Robertson adds, "The sound of revelry by night has no melody to the ears of the man whose wife and children are starving because he does not get a square deal from his employer."

It goes without saying that the soft life and the craving for pleasure is one of the reasons for acquiring riches. How many times have we heard it said, "Money cannot buy happiness," but, how many of us *really do believe* that!

The truth of the matter is James' concluding remarks in verse 5: "you have fattened your hearts in a day of slaughter." This is a quotation from the concepts of Jeremiah 12:3, "...Drag them off like sheep for the slaughter and set them apart for a day of carnage!" Just as a rancher fattens his stock for the packers so the pleasure syndrome is fattening the unsaved rich for the eternal kill. This passage has "an eschatological significance, and...is used of the day of judgment" (Wessel). This is divine irony and sarcasm leveled directly at the follies of the godless rich! God's guns of judgment are aimed and ready. We must never forget that the joy of life is *in* the Lord and not in dollars! The third selfish injustice is seen in:

C. CONDEMNING the Righteous, 5:6. Here is portrayed injustice in its grossest forms. The righteous were being condemned and the wicked were being justified. In the words of James: "You have condemned and put to death the righteous man; he does not resist you" (5:6). Isaiah spoke of this: "Who justify the wicked for a bribe, and take away the rights of the ones who are in the right!" (Isa. 5:23). This was done in many ways in Bible times; but, the primary reference is to the unsaved rich taking the Christian poor to a court of law (James 2:6). There verdicts of condemnation were secured which often resulted in physical death by means of capital punishment. It is certain that the hair on the backs of some of these poor was bristled and they were ready for retaliation.

But the Spirit of Christ was in the hearts of these poor. Paul says, "Never take your own revenge, beloved, but leave room for the wrath of God, for it is written, 'Vengeance is Mine, I will repay, says the Lord' " (Rom. 12:19). Indeed, the human tendency is to lash out and retaliate, which means to inflict like for like. Being mistreated makes one see red anyway. Christ spoke of this avenging process in Matthew 5:38-48. He cited four examples: (1) personal violence (5:39); (2) court litigation (5:40); (3) public exactions (5:41); (4) begging or borrowing (5:42). For an expert treatment on this subject of retaliation, please read *Then Would My Servants Fight* by Dr. Herman A. Hoyt (published by BMH Books).

James was clear that the believing poor practiced the doctrine of non-resistance when he writes: "he does not resist you." Yes, to be unresisting when one is committed to death, as an innocent victim, must demonstrate that one is controlled by the Holy Spirit. The Lord is the Champion of the Christian poor; therefore, he should never allow a spirit of hatred to flare up, but, he must commit his case to God.

There was a church business meeting where an unforgettable experience transpired. An unruly woman stood to her feet and lashed out at the pastor. She accused him falsely and in a blatantly unbiblical manner (Matt. 18:15-17; I Tim. 5:19-20). Her tirade and conduct left much to be desired. Her pastor, later shared with me in confidence, that a spirit of vindictiveness came over him, but the words of Jesus in Matthew 5:39 restrained him from rash retaliation. Then the sweetness of the Holy Spirit, in His calming control, came over the pastor. In a subdued voice that bordered on a monotone, he spoke to her. He said, "Mrs.——, you are not submissive to your husband and that is why he does not attend the church (I Peter 3:1-6). You are not submissive to your pastor-teacher (Heb. 13:17) and that explains this evening's incident. And, it is obvious from this display, that you are not submissive to God and His Word (I Cor. 14:34-35). I publicly commit you to the Lord for His discipline for no one seems to be able to control you." The next day, the woman discovered a growth that killed her six days later. Medically speaking, a tumor cannot grow that fast. Perhaps the growth had been there awhile. At any rate, six days after her physician had discovered it, she died.

God is the Vindicator and God is the Protector. Take your case to Him. The truth is clear: "...do not resist him who is evil; but whoever slaps you on your right cheek, turn to him the other also" (Matt. 5:39). Just as the poor of James 2:6 and 5:6 are totally at the mercy of the unscrupulous, unsaved rich and do not resist, so must you and I. Christ is our Champion, let us take our case to Him. He is the All-powerful One!

Here Comes the Judge

THE CHAPTER OUTLINED:

Many, many times, as I write, I have yearned to speak in a personal way, with my readers. I am sure James also desired to speak face to face with first century kindred after the flesh and after the faith. But, one day soon, that anticipation will become a reality. Yes, dear one, Jesus is coming again (John 14:1-3; Acts 1:11). Therefore, some day in the near future, I *will* see you here, there or in the air! May God be praised!

In a real sense, Christ is the Supreme One. He is coming soon and all of us want His approval. The purpose in this chapter is to kindle a fire of expectancy in hearts for the second coming of Christ. By means of James 5:7-11, may every person be challenged to seek the approval of Jesus Christ whose advent is imminently anticipated.

I. THE EXAMPLE OF THE HARVEST, 5:7

In the first six verses of chapter 5, James has discussed the follies of the love of money and the dangerous activity of the unsaved rich to persecute the saved poor. James again encourages the hearts of the poor brethren by saying their Champion is returning soon!

James says, "Be patient" which comes from a compound word made up of one meaning "long" and another which means "hot anger." The idea therefore is long-tempered and being able to control the passion of anger for a long period of time. The downtrodden poor were exhorted to be patient in the face of the persecutions from their rich oppressors. This patience is called for because of the "therefore." This "therefore" is the note of certainty that the Lord will judge the wicked and vindicate the righteous. It is clear that the attitude of faith is to exhibit *patience* until Christ returns.

James confidently writes, "Be patient, therefore, brethren...." Again, let it be reiterated that the word "therefore" refers back to the Lord's coming which is strongly awaited in 5:1-6 as the time of His reckoning with the unjust. The "Lord of Sabaoth" will then move to vindicate all the suffering of the righteous and demonstrate Himself as the victor and champion these poor brethren have trusted Him to be.

This patience is to be of the duration "until the coming of the Lord." The Greek word translated "coming" is *parousia*. This is the point of climactic realization to which the patient endurance looks, for James mentions it three times (vv. 7, 8, 9). In the last two references, the imminency of this event is a point of emphasis. "...for the coming of the Lord is at hand" (5:8); "...behold, the Judge is standing right at the door" (5:9). In the vernacular, "Here comes the Judge!"

John Walvoord writes:

The word most frequently used in the Scriptures to describe the return of Christ is *parousia*...it occurs twenty-four times in the New Testament...It has come to mean not simply *presence* but the act by which the presence is brought about, that is, by the coming of the individual...Its contribution to the doctrine is to emphasize the bodily presence of Christ.

What is the world coming to?—the second coming of Christ! These early saints were exhorted to watch for it (I Thess. 1:10; 4:13; Titus 2:13). The personal presence of Christ has not occurred yet. Therefore we are to still be waiting and watching (John 14:2-3). Jesus clearly said, in the light of His return, to "Do business with this until I come back" (Luke 19:13). Being busy in the King's business is the necessary activity because of the *parousia*!

The farmer is used as an example of being patient in the middle of difficulties. James is fond of painting pictures and refers often to scenes from nature (1:6, 10-11; 3:3-7, 11; 5:17-18) and farming (1:18; 3:17-18; 5:4, 7). James says, "Behold, the farmer waits for the precious produce of the soil, being patient about it, until it gets the early and late rains." This farmer patiently waits. The happy ending of his patience is the precious produce from the earth. The attitude of the farmer is very much in view. His result is "precious"—meaning of great value and is used that way elsewhere: "but with *precious* blood, as of a lamb unblemished and spotless, the blood of Christ" (I Peter 1:19); "For by these He has granted to us His *precious* and magnificent promises..." (II Peter 1:4). To the hardworking farmer who has undergone the distress of storms, insects, diseases and wild animals, the produce which results is worth waiting for—it is precious. The illustration is clear—it pays to be patient; to wait upon the Lord.

How does the example of the harvest apply to you and me? What does that have to do with our being patient? Peter informs us: "The Lord is not slow about His promise, as some count slowness, but is patient toward you, not wishing for any to perish but for all to come to repentance" (II Peter 3:9). God is patient because He wishes for everyone to come under the sound of the Gospel. The farmer in James 5:7 can be compared to God who is waiting for the precious produce of the soil. God has delayed His coming so that fruit might be produced for the harvest. I am glad He delayed His coming for me! Are you glad or sad?

Saul of Tarsus is a perfect example of God's patience to the foremost of sinners. Saul, before he became the Great Apostle Paul, was a killer of Christians and a blasphemer. He tells Timothy: "It is a truthworthy statement, deserving full acceptance, that Christ Jesus came into the world to save sinners, among whom I am foremost of all. And yet for this reason I found mercy, in order that in me as the foremost, Jesus Christ might demonstrate His perfect patience, as an example for those who would believe in Him for eternal life" (I Tim. 1:15-16).

Another example of the patience of God is seen in "the days of Noah." God allowed Noah to preach for one hundred years before He judged this wicked world. "...when the patience of God kept waiting in the days of Noah, during the construction of the ark, in which a few, that is, eight persons, were brought safely through the water" (I Peter 3:20).

It has been almost two thousand years since He has promised to return. That is a whole lot of patience. But, I might add that His wrath is beginning to boil over, so be ready (Matt. 24:36-39). Greatly similar to the first, is the second reason for patience, which is:

II. THE EXPECTANCY OF HIS SOON RETURN, 5:8

Just like the farmer, who typifies God, "You too be patient; strengthen your hearts, for the coming of the Lord is at hand!" In *Things To Come*, by J. Dwight Pentecost, we read: "The doctrine of imminency is taught in Scripture in such passages as John 14:2-3; I Corinthians 1:7; Philippians 3:20-21; I Thessalonians 1:9-10; 4:16-17; 5:5-9; Titus 2:13; James 5:8-9; Revelation 3:10; 22:17-22."

How imminent is His return? James says that it is "at hand." Paul employs an adverbial form of this same word in Romans 13:11 to say, comparatively, "...for now salvation is *nearer* to us than when we believed."

Because of this imminency, James says, "...strengthen your hearts...." The root form of the word translated "strengthen" means "a prop." The hope of the soon return of Christ is the means whereby we can prop ourselves up. This "blessed hope" should cause the adrenalin to surge through our bodies. He *is* coming soon.

James is saying, under the inspiration of the Holy Spirit, those things that these poor, persecuted brethren needed to hear. If they waited for His coming, they would be able to do two things: (1) *Exercise* self-restraint from retaliation (I Peter 3:20; Gal. 5:22); and (2) *Experience* deliverance from oppression and the judgment of oppressors (Luke 18:7-8; I Thess. 1:10). The third reason for patience is:

III. THE EVALUATION OF THE JUDGE, 5:9

James says "...behold, the Judge is standing right at the door." Again

138   *Studies in James*

a graphic picture is painted to portray the imminency of the Lord's return. "Is standing" is once again in the perfect tense expressing the idea that the coming has drawn near with the present continuing result that it is still drawing nearer. James seems to be echoing the statement of Jesus in Mark 13:29, "...recognize that He is near, right at the door." Added emphasis upon the imminence of Christ's coming is conveyed in James' precise word order: "the Judge right at the door is standing." Christ is right there, ready to take His place in judgment.

Rosscup comments, "The words of verse 9 make it clear that the fact of His coming, though a blessed consolation to inspire patience, is also a basis of warning against impatience." Believers are not to "complain." The verb is in the imperative mood, which issues forth in a resounding command "Stop complaining!" The word means "to groan" (Rom. 8:23; II Cor. 5:2), and when used with *kata* ("against"), as here, "to groan, complain, murmur, grumble, or whine against." Rosscup continues, "It is a common temptation for a man, when facing trying circumstances, to blame others and become irritated or exasperated with them. This is to be impatient rather than patient."

Again James is referring to the "mouth-pieces" of this early *diaspora* congregation. The grumblers were at one another's throats once again. The wisdom from Proverbs applies then and now: "...But he who restrains his lips is wise (10:19); "...But he who repeats a matter separates intimate friends" (17:9); "It is better to live in a corner of a roof, than in a house shared with a contentious woman" (21:9); "It is better to live in a desert land, than with a contentious and vexing woman" (21:19).

The message is simple: Christ is coming soon, so don't be caught complaining. Christ's return is imminent, which means evaluation is imminent. In the words of Paul: "Do all things without grumbling or disputing" (Phil. 2:14). The fourth reason for patience is:

IV. THE EXPERIENCES OF OTHERS, 5:10-11

Exploitation and suffering for righteousness sake is sometimes a bitter pill to swallow. Therefore James selects two Old Testament experiences to illustrate his point. They are:

A. The PATIENCE of the Prophets, 5:10-11. Certainly Jewish believers, who face severe distress, are to be "propped up" by remembering the Old Testament prophets who underwent difficult afflictions, *but* were patient. In fact, the human author asks his Hebrew brethren to perceive these prophets "as an example." This is the first word which James employs in the original word order of verse 10 and therefore becomes the point of emphasis. Ths literal rendering would be: "As an example take, brethren, of suffering and patience, the prophets...."

The Old Testament prophets' examples are noteworthy and therefore should be imitated. It is used, with this meaning throughout Scripture; for example: "Everyone who comes to Me, and hears My words, and acts upon them, I will show you whom he is like" (Luke 6:47). Christ's idea here is to learn under or copy from or imitate. In John 13:15, the words of the Lord are succinct: "For I gave you an example that you should do as I did to you." Here the copy of Christ is to be imitated. The writer of the Hebrews states, "Let us therefore be diligent to enter that rest, lest anyone fall through following the same example of disobedience" (Heb. 4:11). The example here is a warning not to follow the bad example of the Old Testament Israelis who went through the wilderness experience because of their disobedience.

The word "prophets" is in the plural which indicates that God wishes for His sons and daughters to imitate the example of the prophets in the entire panorama of the prophetic period. All of the prophets, who suffered for Jehovah, cannot be included in a book such as this. Therefore, let us consider several examples:

1. Jeremiah was known as "the weeping prophet." He certainly is the most notable for his endurance in severe trials, which were numerous.

2. Elijah spoke of the killing of God's prophets (I Kings 19:10, 14; II Kings 9:7).

3. Nehemiah writes of this "prophetcide," when he says, "But they became disobedient and rebelled against Thee, and cast Thy law behind their backs and killed Thy prophets who had admonished them so that they might return to Thee, and they committed great blasphemies " (Neh. 9:26).

4. Christ Himself prepared His disciples when He uttered, "Blessed are those who have been persecuted for the sake of righteousness, for theirs is the kingdom of heaven. Blessed are you when men revile you, and persecute you, and say all kinds of evil against you falsely, on account of Me. Rejoice, and be glad, for your reward in heaven is great, for so they persecuted the prophets who were before you" (Matt. 5:10-12).

5. Stephen stood before the Council and charged unbelieving Israel with: "Which one of the prophets did your fathers not persecute? And they killed those who had previously announced the coming of the Righteous One, whose betrayers and murderers you have now become" (Acts

7:52).

These Old Testament prophets "spoke in the name of the Lord." James is simply reiterating what poor, suffering Jeremiah said in 20:9, as he lamented his trials, "But if I say, 'I will not remember Him or speak any more *in His name*'; then in my heart it becomes like a burning fire shut up in my bones; and I am weary of holding it in, and I cannot endure it." When one speaks in "the name of the Lord" he speaks in the very authority of the Lord. Needless to say, this can become somewhat unsettling to the one who lives outside of God. The Word of God causes conviction and conviction can generate into anger and anger can kill a prophet of God.

Have you ever considered the mentality of a critic? For example, why would a man murder a prophet? Because the prophet says what convicts, and it is easier to kill the prophet than change the life. Symptoms are much easier to deal with than the problems which cause the symptoms. The mentality of a critic is seen, when money is discussed in church services. The one who criticizes the request for money is *not* a giver. Givers are never bothered by monetary discussions. The critic is the one who doesn't give and his criticism reveals that he is convicted about it. Witnessing is another case. May I suggest that the person who is critical of aggressive evangelism is one who is *not* sharing his faith in Christ. The mentality of the critic is simply to put down or eliminate that which bothers him, and therefore to arrive at some kind of comfort zone in order to excuse his lack of performance.

That is why Old Testament prophets were killed. That is why the Apostles were all martyred except John. That is why these *diaspora* believers, who were contemporary with James, were suffering at the hands of oppressors. You see, Christianity has always bothered the critic, for it confronts the critic with his need for change. Criticism is more comfortable than change!

Contrasted to the resentful grumbling or whining self-pity described in verse 9, these Christians are exhorted to lift up their heads triumphantly by the grace of God. As my eighth grade coach used to say, "Keep your head up, son! Play proud!" Indeed, the believer can be proud (or rather confident) in the sufficiency of his Christ. That is what James has in mind when he begins the eleventh verse with the participle "Behold." He says, "Stop, look and listen for we count those completely adequate in Christ [blessed] who endured!"

"Blessed" is a great and beautiful word. It means happy. That really grabs me at the heartstrings! Those who endure for Christ are happy. The present tense adds further force to the power of this statement. The habitual status of these suffering saints is happiness. This is shades of Daniel 12:12, "How blessed is he who keeps waiting...." The words of Christ on blessedness are also of great moment (Matt. 5:3-11). One who is under the gun of continual pressure can be continually happy through resources in Christ that are adequate.

B. The PATIENCE of Job, 5:11. James has brought to mind the prophets who endured and whose state was happiness. These were the clergymen; the seminary graduates; the "professionals" so to speak. Now he cites a layman, who is *the* outstanding, dynamic example of a man who suffered, endured and was supremely blessed afterward. Job is the man and he was sorely tried!

The expert exegete, Spiros Zodiates says of Job:

> The people whom James addresses had surely heard of the patience of Job. He was the classic example of patience. They undoubtedly knew his own story and could readily understand that he did not deserve what he went through. During his ordeal much sympathy was expressed on the part of his family and friends. How could one help but feel sorry for him, who had lost all his possessions and all his children and who suffered so much pain in his ailing body? Job complained a great deal. He even wished that he had never been born. Yet his imperfections and human weaknesses are scarcely remembered. Only his patience is spoken of. This is very characteristic of God's long-suffering toward his saints. How terrible it would be if all that God could remember us for were our failings and our weaknesses...People tend to remember the bad things about us, but God remembers the good things.

Job tersely relates, "Though He slay me, I will hope in Him. Nevertheless I will argue my ways before Him" (Job 13:15). Sometimes his mouth got in the way (cf. Job. 3:3, 11; 7:11-16; 10:18; 16:2; 23:2; 30:20-23), but Job was patient and trusted and endured. So, it is written of him, "And the Lord restored the fortunes of Job when he prayed for his friends, and the Lord increased all that Job had twofold" (Job 42:10). The fifth reason to patiently wait for the Lord's approval is:

V. THE END OF THE LORD'S DEALINGS, 5:11

James continues, "...and have seen the outcome of the Lord's dealings...." The word "outcome" or "end" carries two meanings in Scripture: (1) "end" in the sense of the last part or final act in some process, as I Corinthians 15:24; (2) "purpose," that is, the actual aim or goal which

God appointed and then worked to accomplish, as I Timothy 1:5. Arndt and Gingrich in their masterpiece lexicon take it in the second sense, which is better in this context anyway.

Of course, the goal or aim or purpose for us is to be busy for Christ in the light of His soon return. The next item on God's prophetic agenda is the rapture of the church. It may occur at any moment! Do you realize, fellow worker for Christ, that you and I may soon be a part of a select group of people who will never die! Can you imagine being a part of the rapture? That will make us celebrities in heaven along with Enoch and Elijah! Conceive of Paul walking up to you and saying, "How does it feel never to have died?" Are you ready?

We close our chapter with James' conclusion of the eleventh verse, "...that the Lord is full of compassion and is merciful." Christ is aware of the plight of those who love Him. He is "full of compassion" or "brimming with kindness." He is also "merciful" meaning His heart is full of pity. Friends, He loves us—He knows and He cares! Let us endure for He has endured us and for us!

When You Have Your Health, You Have Just About Everything (Part I)

If you ask some people, "How are you?"—they reply with an "organ recital." They give a complete dissertation on livers, hearts, bladders, kidneys or whatever! They are like a mini-hypochondriac ward! In this section, we are not discussing the chronic complainer, but the one who is seriously ill, indeed.

It is important to have the "Divine Perspective" on illness. There is much misunderstanding on sickness, the atonement, and the common man as is evidenced even in the charismatic cults. The need of the hour is—what does the Bible teach and not what "Sister Serena" or "Mother Mongus" have to say!

God is in favor of healing and so am I! But it is critical to gain God's methodology and God's viewpoint if we are to know and correctly understand the subject of healing. The purpose in this chapter is to acquire illumination and enlightenment from the Scriptures on the subject of healing. What does the Bible teach concerning healing?

I. THE PATTERN IN THE CHURCH TODAY

We are living in a day of error and counterfeits. Christ predicted that satanic delusions would be omnipresent, in the last days, which would include false Christs and false prophets demonstrating many demonic signs and wonders (Mark 13:22) and deceive many. Paul warned that "the mystery of lawlessness is already at work" (II Thess. 2:7). And at the end of the church age, lawlessness will cause to "fall away from the faith, paying attention to deceitful spirits and doctrines of demons" (I Tim. 4:1).

Paul also warned that "Satan disguises himself as an angel of light" (II Cor. 11:14). God's people are capable of demonic delusions by means of false teachers. John reiterates, "Beloved, do not believe every spirit, but test the spirits to see whether they are from God; because many false prophets have gone out into the world" (I John 4:1).

Unger writes:

> The power to heal diseases is frequently manifested in spiritism, magic, and demon possession. The clairvoyant medium often claims that he can heal the body, as well as foretell the future. The magical charmer and mesmerizer can both cure and cause diseases. The person afflicted with an evil spirit is often promised ability to cure physical aliments if he will serve the dominating demon.
>
> Because of the satanic imitation of the genuine "gifts of healing" (I Cor. 12:9), it is imperative and of the utmost importance that God's people dismiss the naive and erroneous notion that all healings are of God. God's children need the gift of "discerning of spirits" (I

Cor. 12:10) to beware of occult healing methods and similar movements of our day. Otherwise they run the risk of being seduced by religiously camouflaged acts where the demonic masquerades as the divine.

Without mincing words, the cultic type of healing meetings in auditoriums and tents is *not* Biblical! There is no scriptural warrant for it at all! As I was going through high school and college, as a young convert to Christ, I would attend so-called healing meetings. I was present where one man, in downtown Los Angeles, claimed to have the fountain of youth in his church. The elderly were in single file awaiting their anointing from this fountain. It was promised them, that in direct proportion to the amount of money they gave, their lives would be lenghtened. The coffers were overflowing that night.

The radio advertised that on a certain Friday, a four hundred pound, fat lady was, by the healing power of God, going to reduce before your very eyes. I attended, but that lady was held up in traffic and never arrived (even after the "rush hour on the freeways").

II. A PANORAMA OF GOD'S TRUTH

The gifts of healings were part of the program of God in the apostolic church era. Out of the gifts which God gave to the church (I Cor. 12 and Rom. 12), were four miracle gifts. These gifts were not for the church, but for unbelievers to confirm to them the authenticity of the message of the apostles and prophets. These four gifts are: (1) Miracles, (2) Healings, (3) Tongues, and (4) The Interpretation of Tongues. They have no continuing role in the church; but, existed for the apostolic times, designed to confirm divine revelation before the New Testament canon was completed and while God was still directly doing signs in the face of Israel. Let me suggest their nature from several passages.

(If you find yourself in disagreement with me, let me remind you that what I am saying I am saying in love. After innumerable hours of study, I am presenting to you what I believe the Bible teaches. I might add that precious friends of mine are charismatic cultists and exponents of the miracle gifts. I, therefore, have endeavored to be Biblically objective. I have prayed that God would guide me beyond my blind spots).

Mark 16:14-18 says that the emissaries of Christ would have attendant miracles. If we are to assume that someone has all of this in the contemporary church, then we must agree with the Appalachian Snake Handlers and the Church of the First Born, wherein we drink poison (most of the time to our demise). If we take part of this, then we must take all of it.

In II Corinthians 12:12 it speaks of "the signs of a true apostle . . . ." The definite article "the" depicts specific signs and not some signs. This is a reference to *the* definite identification of specific signs given *only* to apostles. Apparently these are those signs granted back in Mark 6.

Hebrews 2:3 says, "How shall we escape if we neglect so great a salvation? After it was at the first spoken through the Lord, it was *confirmed* to us by those who heard." It is very important to realize that the entire Book of Hebrews was written wholly to Jews. What was *affirmed* was *confirmed*! How? Verse 4 answers, "God also bearing witness with them, both by signs and wonders and by various miracles and by gifts of the Holy Spirit according to His own will." These specific gifts of the Holy Spirit were to confirm the Word of God in the hearing of these Jews. Therefore, these gifts have their significance in the apostolic ministry, which was, incidentally, a foundational ministry!

B.B. Warfield adds:

> These miracle gifts were part of the credentials of the apostles, as the authoritative agents of God, in founding the church. Their function distinctly confirmed them to the apostolic church and they necessarily passed away with it.

Now, if we believe that Ephesians 2:20 says that the apostles and prophets were the foundation, then the signs of an apostle faded out when the apostles passed from existence. And, if the signs of an apostle were the confirming gifts of the Holy Spirit, then the whole thing comes together; and it is clear that when the apostles went, so did the gifts of the Spirit.

The church today *does not need* the miracle gift confirmation! The standard is the Bible. To say that we need apostolic signs is to overlook the finality of Scriptures. Luke 16:31 and the Epistles continually say, "Teach sound doctrine!"

Therefore, in our consideration of only one of the four miracle gifts; namely, the gifts of healing (I Cor. 12:9), let it be firmly understood—God *does* heal the sick! But the gifts of healing are not in existence today, because apostles do not exist today. In James 5:12-20, it is clear that God has a plan for healing and that the gifts of healing do not have any particular relationship to the church at all.

Even the speaking in tongues phenomena involved a direct purpose to Israel. It was a miracle that God used to confirm the Word. The most important thing that happened in Acts 2 was Peter's preaching. It was a tremendous sermon. One sermon…and three thousand people were saved. Today, it seems that many poor preachers must preach three thousand sermons to get one person saved. At any rate, three thousand people repented in Acts 2. The tongues episode confirmed in the minds of these Jews that Peter's sermon was from God. Speaking in tongues was a sign only for Jews. It has no significance for Gentiles. It is presented this way all through the Book of Acts. Therefore, in the modern church, when believers exercise tongues together, it is totally anti-Biblical.

It is clear from I Corinthians 14:21 (which is a quotation from Isaiah 28:11) that the purpose of tongues was to Israel! God spoke to His chosen people by means of a miracle of the mouth. Tongues never had any meaning for believers. That was the whole problem in Corinth. Those Gentile believers were exalting tongues. In I Corinthians 14:22 it explicitly states: "So then, tongues are for a sign, not to those who believe, but to unbelievers...." The Corinthians were majoring in the minors. They confused the sign gift of tongues with the oracles in their Greek religious background. In their pagan worship there was ecstatic speech. Paul is trying to correct the problem without totally eliminating tongues because a large contingency of Jews were still in the Grecian city of Corinth. Paul knows there will be occasions when tongues can be used to confirm the Word to an unbelieving Jew.

Therefore, the total tongues movement, which is in vogue today, is not sanctioned by the New Testament. Today we are told by the charismatics, that we don't have all that God wants to give. They say the fullness of the Holy Spirit can be experienced only by speaking in tongues. Therefore, Gentile believers are doing it to each other. So, Paul says in I Corinthians 14:23-26 to try preaching for believers, for that is what *they* need! He tells the Corinthians that they don't need any more experience, they need doctrine! In the Scriptures, one will experience all the experience that there is to experience!

Again, it is clear from I Corinthians 14:23 that the miracle gifts (including tongues), were signs to the *Jews* who believe *not*! Corinth was a Greek city full of Gentiles. Gentile unbelievers were coming to the church services and they thought that the tongues-speakers had flipped out and were nuts! They were being exposed to something that God never intended for a Gentile.

In A.D. 70, Titus Vespasian destroyed the city of Jerusalem and dispersed the Jews to the four corners of the earth. At that point, in fulfillment of the prophecy of Christ (Matt. 24:1-2), God terminated His dealings with the Jews who had rejected their Messiah. God turned to the Gentiles (Rom. 9–11). By that very fact alone, the miracle gifts had to cease. God is no longer in the business of giving special signs to Israel. He has temporarily set them aside and judicially blinded them.

Even in the latter years of the apostolic era, these gifts began to wane. Paul told Timothy, "...but use a little wine for the sake of your stomach and your *frequent ailments*" (I Tim. 5:23). Why didn't Paul tell Timothy to go to an auditorium or a tent? Why didn't Paul heal Timothy? Listen to Paul again, "...but Trophimus I left sick at Miletus" (II Tim. 4:20). If healers were around, why didn't Paul prescribe one for poor Trophimus? Why didn't Paul heal him before he left Miletus? It is obvious that the apostolic era was drawing to a close. There also seems to be no case in the New Testament where this gift is exercised toward a believer. The Biblical directives toward healing must be understood in their proper perspective and context.

Dear friend, the idea that some people can heal in an assembly-line fashion is non-Biblical. If they really had the gift of healing, they would be in hospitals, not in tents, and they would be going to unbelievers and preaching the Gospel and confirming the Word to them.

We must never overlook the fact that sometimes sickness serves a very constructive function. Paul is a classic example of this truth. He entreated the Lord three times to be healed (II Cor. 12:7-10), probably from an Oriental eye disease. Three times his requests were denied. The divine reasons were simple: "And because of the surpassing greatness of the revelations, for this reason, to keep me from exalting myself....For when I am weak, then I am strong." Why didn't Paul heal himself? God was fulfilling His purposes through Paul's sickness.

The basic, New Testament teaching on healing is embodied in the James passage before us. Spliced within it is also a statement on the swearing of an oath. A word is in order concerning:

III. A PERSPECTIVE ON NONSWEARING, 5:12

The ancient Jews were big on the swearing of oaths. Remember, James is very practical and he is going to slam fearlessly into problems of his contemporaries. These Hebrew saints were being persecuted for their faith. They were vulnerable for satanic attack. It was open season on Christians and they were viable targets for demonic assault. Not only was Satan instigating persecution, he was also counterfeiting the gifts of healing as well as all the miracle gifts.

Dr. Louis S. Bauman in *The Faith* makes three observations about the doctrine of nonswearing. I paraphrase them in the following: (1) the taking of an oath is plain disobedience to the commands of Jesus—Matthew

5:33-37, I John 2:3-5, Luke 6:46; (2) the oath is the strength of secret darkness; (3) the very atmosphere of the oath-bound secret society is deadly to the real spiritual life of a Christian—II Corinthians 6:14-18.

Satan is strong enough without our assisting him by binding ourselves with an oath. James postulates quite tersely, "But above all, my brethren, do not swear, either by heaven or by earth or with any other oath; but let your yes be yes, and your no, no; so that you may not fall under judgment" (James 5:12). For a very good and a much fuller discussion of this subject, may I refer the reader to Dr. Herman A. Hoyt's book, *All Things Whatsoever I Have Commanded You* (published by BMH Books, Winona Lake, Indiana).

To conclude the thoughts on nonswearing for our purposes in this chapter, permit me to cite a quotation from the book mentioned above. Dr. Hoyt writes:

> Swearing is the calling upon a higher power to guarantee the speaking of truth, at the same time invoking terrible penalty for failure to do so. This was practiced during Old Testament times, but our Lord, with sovereign authority, abrogated the whole system and insisted that for Christians the simple affirmation of truth was sufficient. There is not even provision made for swearing by God.

James moves to verses 13 and 14 in:

IV. THE PROCEDURE TO FOLLOW, 5:13-14

To sort of bring things to a head, let the reader once again be aware that James is a most practical book and it touches on many aspects of the game of life. To this point in his book, he has been addressing Jewish converts who were under severe persecution. He has pressed home the attitude of faith toward the circumstances of life. This walk of faith commits matters to God in prayer (James 5:13); it considers it all joy because the resources in Christ are adequate (James 4:6); it looks to a Lord who "will exalt you" (James 4:10). Christ is ready to help in the here and now and in the hereafter when He makes all the wrong things right!

Faith inevitably expresses itself through prayer, which enables a man to take on life with patience, whatever his particular experience. It prompts him to look to God with a heart receptive to Him and His gifts of blessing. This is true for a believer whether his situation at the moment is one of affliction or merriment (James 5:13); sickness (James 5:14-15); sin; or ministering for the uplifting of a brother who is in sin (James 5:15-20). James has placed an emphasis upon prayer (1:5-8, 4:2-3 and in the passage before us, 5:13-18). The procedure for us to follow:

A. In Relation to SUFFERING, 5:13. The question posed "Is anyone among you suffering?" It means "to suffer hardship or evil, be vexed or troubled" (II Tim. 2:9), or, sometimes, "bear hardship patiently" (II Tim. 2:3; 4:5). James employs the noun form in 5:10 for the prophets suffering of affliction. This may be physical or mental and can include a wide range of troubles that would be involved in testings of believers (1:2-12).

When the believer is suffering, "Let him pray." The word "pray" is in the imperative form of the verb and therefore shows that we are commanded to pray. It is as Luke records, "Now He was telling them a parable to show that at all times they ought to pray and not to lose heart" (Luke 18:1). Prayer is not an optional matter. Zodiates comments:

> The afflictions of this world should cause us to lift our hearts up to God. Let us not turn to any human being when we are under pressure from the evil of this world, but depend upon God, for that is where we are supposed to be driven, and nowhere else.

Obviously our prayers, among other things, should include request for wisdom (James 1:5) so that we might look at the circumstances with God's perspective. Heaven knows how we need it!

B. In Relation to CHEERFULNESS, 5:13. "Is anyone cheerful?" It is used also in Acts 27:22, 25 and means "in good spirits or mind." The idea is that the believer is encouraged and exuberant.

Rosscup comments:

> The implication may be that he is temporarily free from adversity and therefore feeling in good spirits. Thus it would be in contrast to the previous phrase in 13. However, it also can mean that he is courageously cheerful even while still in trouble because he sees or hears some particular aspect that encourages (Acts 24:10; 27:36) or because he simply encourages himself in the Lord despite the circumstances. Paul and Silas are the illustrations of this last case as they sing in the Philippian jail when their situation itself is gloomy (Acts 16).

"Let him sing praises" is the translation of only one Greek word, *psalleto*. It can mean, as in the Old Testament, to sing to the accompaniment of a harp, and this would usually involve a psalm written for this use (Rom. 15:9; I Cor. 14:15,26). But it can also mean simply to sing praise, not necessarily in a psalm, for it could be in any of the categories of "speaking to one another in psalms and hymns and spiritual songs, singing and making melody with your heart to the Lord" (Eph. 5:19). One sings in praise, accompanied by the chords of the heart. This singing fits into the emphasis upon *prayer* in the context, for it is, in essence, one form of vocalizing praise to God as in prayer.

C. In Relation to SICKNESS, 5:14. James asks, "Is anyone among you sick?" Another word for sick appears in verse 15. According to Arndt and Gingrich in their *Greek-English Lexicon of the New Testament and Other Early Christian Literature*, the root word has a meaning wider than simply sickness. It can refer to one who is:

1. Weak in the economical sense of poverty or need (Acts 20:35).
2. Weak in the sense of being over-scrupulous in regard to understanding liberty in Christ (Rom. 14:2, 21; I Cor. 8:11ff).
3. Weakness in the sense of inability, as the law was weak through the flesh (Rom. 8:3), and Paul was weak in himself apart from grace (II Cor. 12:10).
4. Weak in the sense of bodily sickness (Acts 9:37; Phil. 2:26; II Tim. 4:20, and so forth).

The above fourth meaning is by far the more frequent meaning. The fourth sense is evidently in view in James 5:14.

Now, these sick people are "to call for the elders of the church...." How many times has a pastor been criticized because he didn't call at someone's home? It is clear from this fourteenth verse, that if a pastor is needed, he is to be called. Rosscup adds:

> It is the responsibility of the ailing person to call for the elders. In many cases today, sick members of the church blame the pastor or others in responsible positions because they have not "shown enough concern to visit," yet nobody has bothered about the detail of letting these people know. How was the pastor supposed to know—by mental telepathy or by angelic vision?

It is also significant that the word for "elders" (*presbuterous*) is plural in number. The New Testament congregations did not have only one pastor like modern congregations. It was not a one man show. This is one reason why so many contemporary churches are small, ineffective and dying—simply disobedience. The Bible says that there is to be a plurality of elders (Acts 15:6, 22; 20:17; 21:18; Phil. 1:1). Why do so many churches "hire" one man, make him do all the work, thus killing him and the church?

The word "church" is used by James for the first time in the epistle. He used the word synagogue in chapter 2 referring to the place where these Hebrew Christians of the *diaspora* met for worship. A church is a "called out" group of people who adhere to Christ and His teachings.

When these elders are summoned, they are to "pray over him, anointing him with oil in the name of the Lord."

Again, it is no secret how much I have appreciated the scholarship of Dr. James E. Rosscup, under whose tutelage I sat in the seminary classroom.

In brief, oil did have therapeutic value in ancient times as well as today, but it is best to understand it here as a symbol of God's miraculous work in healing.

That it had good medicinal effects is clear. It possessed soothing and curative value for animals, like sheep (Ps. 23:5), and men (Isa. 1:6). The good Samaritan in Christ's parable applied oil to the wounds of the man he helped (Luke 10:34). There are numerous instances of its use in extra-Biblical sources (cf. Mayor, pp. 170ff; Mitton, p. 198; Plummer, p. 328). But it is not the meaning of James for various reasons. Though it was a therapeutic aid in some cases, it would not be a cure in all sicknesses in general. Further, James does not say in v. 15 that the oil will cure the sick or even that the oil plus the prayer will make him well. Specifically, he does say that "the prayer of faith shall save the sick," and makes no claim for the oil. It is not the oil but the Lord who "shall raise him up." There is also another factor. In the event that the oil were merely medicinal would not *one* elder be sufficient to apply it, and not elders (plural)?

It is more adequate to say that the anointing is for the purpose of symbolizing tangibly the setting apart of the man to the miraculous healing work of God. It would be an aid to his faith by prompting a sense of expectancy. Christ Himself applied saliva to men at times evidently to symbolize, by physical contact, the healing that God would effect (Mark 7:33; 8:23). There is Old Testament support for the idea that the anointing could signify the *setting apart* of the man to God for His will and operation. There are numerous applications of oil not to cure but to set apart or identify things or persons with God in some sense. Jacob anointed the stone at Bethel to identify it as symbolizing the "house of God" in which he had been a guest (Gen. 28:18; 31:13). When he poured oil upon it, it was not to make it well! It was a ceremonial custom later to anoint priests (Exod. 18:41; 29:7; Lev. 8:12), prophets (I Kings 19:16), and kings (I Sam. 9:10; 10:1; I Kings 19:15). This was to symbolize that they were set apart to and identified with God for His will. When Jesus sent out the twelve disciples, they "anointed with oil many that were sick, and healed them" (Mark 6:13).

(The reader is asked to please turn to chapter 13 for the second half of our discussion of James 5:12-20).

13

When You Have Your Health, You Have Just About Everything [Part II]

THE CHAPTER OUTLINED:

V. The **POWER** That Heals, 5:15

    A. It Is a Prayer of **WORSHIP**

    B. It Is a Prayer According to the **WILL** of God

    C. It Is Prayer Concerned with the **WORK** of God

VI. The **PERSONNEL** God Uses, 5:16-18

    A. One Another, 5:16

    B. A Righteous Man, 5:16

    C. Elijah, 5:17-18

VII. The **PURPOSES** for God Bringing Sickness, 5:19-20

VIII. A **POSTSCRIPT** on Healing

God *is* still in the healing business. But the gifts of healing are no longer given to individual people. God has set down in His Book the correct procedure for divine healing. This is embodied in the words of James 5:12-20. Prayer is powerful and should always be the prevalent pattern of the believer's heart. This is part of God's healing procedure. Then the elders take part in very serious cases of sickness, which we shall discuss in this chapter.

What does the Bible teach concerning healing? Continuing from the last chapter is:

V. THE POWER THAT HEALS, 5:15

The anointing has already taken place at this point of the narrative as the tense of the participle in verse 14 implies. As L. L. Grubb writes,

> Let the elders anoint the sick one with oil in the name of the Lord Jesus Christ....Oil in Scripture is a symbol of the Holy Spirit. Thus, the anointing simply symbolizes the coming of the Holy Spirit in the name of Jesus Christ and in power to perform His office work. He, not oil, does the healing. Even Christ healed through the Spirit (Matt. 12:28).

James says in the fifteenth verse, "and the prayer offered in faith will restore the one who is sick, and the Lord will raise him up, and if he has committed sins, they will be forgiven him." The phrase could better be translated, "And the prayer of the faith..." "The faith" is a term which denotes the sum total of God's Word and will as contained in the Bible. Jude uses the term in the sense, "Beloved, while I was making every effort to write you about our common salvation, I felt the necessity to write to you appealing that you contend earnestly for *the faith* which was once for all delivered to the saints" (Jude 3).

Therefore, the prayer that is in view is a prayer that is unique to the Christian *faith*. It is a prayer which issues forth out of the total body of revelation recorded in the Bible. There are three observations about this unique prayer that I wish to make:

A. It is a Prayer of WORSHIP. Dr. Herman A. Hoyt contributes: "This is a prayer of worship and devotion, as the Greek word implies, and not a prayer of demand." There is a word for demand and this is not that word. Therefore this prayer is uttered in absolute humility before God and in a deep sense of adoration toward Him.

B. It is a Prayer According to the WILL of God. "The faith" is the sum total of Christian belief. This prayer is in harmony with that; therefore, it is in harmony with God. Prayer, which is in conformity to the will of God, is prayer that will be granted. John reinforces this, "And this is the confidence which we have before Him, that, if we ask anything according to His will, He hears us. And if we know that He hears us in whatever we ask, we know that we have the requests which we have asked from Him" (I John 5:14-15). Dr. Donald W. Burdick summarizes,

The order of John's reasoning in these two verses (14-15) is as follows: (1) we ask in accordance with God's will; (2) we therefore know that God listens favorably to our request; and (3) thus we know that the request is granted to us. The basic assurance is that God grants requests for things which are in agreement with His will.

Is it always the will of God to heal? (For a very good treatment of this subject, may I recommend the booklet by Dr. Charles W. Mayes, *Is Healing in the Atonement?* published by BMH Books). For the purposes of our discussion here, my answer is that it is not always the will of God for healing to take place. For example, Paul did not heal Pastor Epaphroditus. He writes in Philippians 2:27, "For indeed he was sick to the point of death, but God had mercy on him, and not on him only but also on me, lest I should have sorrow upon sorrow." Paul yearned for Epaphroditus' healing, but it was not the will of God! Paul left Trophimus at Miletus sick as reported in II Timothy 4:20. Paul had the gift of healing but he could not exercise it toward Trophimus because it was not the will of God! Paul is the classic example, because he could not heal himself because it was not the will of God (II Cor. 12:7-9).

In the words of Dr. Hoyt:

This word of caution should be added. While nothing is said about using the services of a doctor, certainly nothing in the passage prevents it. It may be that God will heal through the medium of medical attention. This may be the means God will use in answering the prayer of the elders. It is wise at least to employ every good means. And it is good theology to remember that while God may will and order the end, He also uses means to reach the desired end. Above all things believers should not limit God by making it impossible for Him to use medical skill....But a prayer that is according to the will of God is also one of personal faith, and in this case personal faith on the part of the elders. God not only supplies the foundation for faith, but gives faith to place on the foundation (Eph. 2:8-9). And God honors such faith.

C. It is a Prayer Concerned with the WORK of God. This prayer does not come from man, but God. God is working through the elders in this prayer (James 5:16). Therefore, it is God's power and not the elders' power.

This prayer "will restore the one who is sick." This is not a blue-sky-come-on promise; but, the affirmation of a fact. Even the prayer is the work of God as the context argues. Note the last half of verse 16, "The effective prayer of a righteous man can accomplish much." It appears, that because the man in verse 16 is righteous, God will grant the request. But, this is not the thrust at all. Dr. Hoyt adds:

> But upon closer investigation it will be found that the Greek participle rendered "effectual fervent" (KJV) has been construed as a middle voice, whereas the other 18 uses of the same word in the New Testament, the same form is always passive. This leads one to believe that it should read, "The prayer of a righteous man, which is energized (wrought) in him, accomplishes much." This reading makes the value of the prayer depend upon God, who energizes the prayer in the elders.

Philippians 2:13 seems to verify Dr. Hoyt's point, "For it is God who is at work in you, both to will and to work for His good pleasure."

This unique prayer, which embodies the sum total of the faith, and which is wrought by God "will restore the one who is sick." The verb translated "will restore" (sosei) is a future active of the root sozo, which means to make well. Dr. A. T. Robertson writes concerning this word: "As in Matthew 9:21ff; Mark 6:56. No reference here to salvation of the soul. The medicine does not heal the sick, but it helps nature (God) do it."

The work of God is seen not only in His giving the proper prayer, but also by the phrase, "...and the Lord will raise him up." The verb is also future active and as Robertson says again, "Precious promise, but not for a professional 'faith-healer' who scoffs at medicine and makes merchandise out of prayer."

The last half of verse 15 gives another work of God, "and if he has committed sins, they will be forgiven him." "If" introduces a third-class condition. For the sake of argument, James states that it is supposed that he has been involved in sins of commission and/or omission as is the case with some others who were sick in the New Testament (Mark 2:5ff; John 5:14; 9:2ff; I Cor. 11:30). Dr. Hoyt, in his usual clear style, says:

> It is implied, although it is not specifically stated, that personal sins may be the cause of the illness. They sometimes are (John 5:14). And where personal sin is the cause of sickness, those sins must be confessed and put away, if healing is to come from the Lord. Confession of sin will bring the saint into a new light and place of blessing with the Lord. He will catch a new vision of the Lord and will see sin in its blackness as never before.

Where personal sin is not the cause of sickness, this service will provide an opportunity for the sick person to consider anew the holiness of the Lord and the sinfulness of sin, and will be one factor in bringing him closer to the Lord. Confessing faults one to another is not an enjoyable thing, but it leads to humility and mutual concern for one another which expresses itself in prayer.

Whenever sin is confessed, whether it is the cause of the sickness or not, it will be forgiven (I John 1:9). If it is the cause of the sickness, the cause being removed, healing will follow. But best of all, the sin being removed will bring the believer into a new appreciation of the fellowship with his fellow Christians and with the Lord Jesus Christ. There is nothing more precious than this. If this service will accomplish this for the saint, he can well thank the Lord that He allowed sickness to come into his life.

Dear reader, the power of God is still available! The Lord has power to heal, praise His name! The oil is symbolic of the Holy Spirit and the anointing service is God's provision coupled with prayer, for healing. It works. As a pastor-teacher, I am an elder, and I have been involved in numerous bedside anointings. I have witnessed God work in marvelous ways. Sometimes He grants a healing and sometimes He doesn't. But, the important thing to remember is that the Lord may *will* a healing or He may *will* a sickness (John 9:3). What He wills is what we must accept. But, the point is still clear that God has given a provision for healing to His people; namely, prayer and anointing of oil. God is able! In the words of Paul, "Now to Him who is able to do exceedingly abundantly beyond all that we ask or think, according to the power that works within us" (Eph. 3:20). Now we come to:

VI. THE PERSONNEL GOD USES, 5:16-18

We see three cases where God used people, both in the present and in the past. These are:

A. One Another, 5:16. The ministry of the body of Christ to each other is also seen in the Book of James, and especially here in verse 16. These beautiful brethren, who had their share of problems, are exhorted to: "confess your sins to one another, and pray for one another." These two things are clear:

1. Confession, 5:16. The word "confess" can be understood in the following ways: first, there are sins that must be acknowledged before God. Second, these sins may be sins which are between individuals and should be settled according to the method outlined in Matthew 18:15-17. Third, confession may need to be made before the entire fellowship of believers of that specific locality. If a person has sinned against the body or that body is universally aware of the particular sin, then confession needs to be public. The tense of the verb confess is present and the attitude of confession therefore is to be habitual. The media says we never outgrow our need for milk, which may or may not be true. But, one thing is sure and that is we never outgrow our need for confession. The second ministry of the body is seen in verse 16:

2. Prayer, 5:16. I don't know where the concept came from that the pastor is the only "minister," but it did *not* come from God! No wonder so many churches are small, weak and ineffective, they have only *one minister*! Ephesians 4:11-16 is quite clear that the pastor is not even to do the work of service, the people are. He is to train the members of the body to minister to each other. If this is done, then the congregation will have as many ministers as they do *members*—everyone ministering one to another. Do you have any idea what kind of power a *ministry* like that could unleash?

This concept is seen again in verse 16—members are praying for members. In other words, people are ministering to people. My friend and colleague, Dr. David L. Hocking, lists eight important representative areas of the body's responsibility of each to the other:

    a. Bearing one another's burdens—Galatians 6:2.
    b. Teaching and admonishing one another—Colossians 3:16.
    c. Using hospitality one toward another—I Peter 4:8-9.
    d. Comforting one another—I Thessalonians 4:18; 5:11.
    e. Forgiving one another—Ephesians 4:32; Colossians 3:13.
    f. Restoring a sinning brother—Galatians 6:1.
    g. Spending time with one another—Hebrews 10:24-25.
    h. Loving one another—John 13:34-35; I Peter 1:22; I John 4:7.

There is no way that one "minister" or pastor can do all of the above for every member of the fellowship of believers—no way! He might be able to if he leads a little, tiny church. But that little, tiny church is doomed to stay little, tiny if only one person does the work of service. (But, I am sorry to report that there really are people who want to keep their churches small. Perhaps to them, being a big fish in a small pond is some kind of ego trip.) To believe that one man can do the work of ministering is the height of absurdity and Biblical illiteracy.

James is very clear when he says that one of the works of service is praying for one another. Dearly beloved, do you realize how important it is to pray for one another? The importance is revealed in just this one word "pray" used by James. It is a present imperative, which means that you and I, Christian, are commanded by God to pray for each other!

Not only are we commanded, but the present tense instructs us to pray all the time! (I Thess. 5:17). I don't think that we need to be reminded that failure to comply with this command is an act of disobedience. All disobedience is sin and one cannot expect the blessing of God on his life unless he is willing to obey God. Dear friend, I predict that if you removed the incredible burden of your pastor's ministering to everybody, and disbursed this function to every member of your church, your fellowship of believers would triple in size in one year!

At any rate, James says, "Pray for one another." The purpose of this praying is also carefully spelled out in the clause, "so that you may be healed." Is it possible for a humble believer to be involved in a healing of another humble believer apart from a pastor or a divine healer? Yes, indeed! Here is just such a situation.

Are you desirous of changing a situation (like a healing or an unsaved loved one's conversion)? Then take a lesson from Hannah in I Samuel 1:1-20. Hannah was in a very bad predicament. She was barren and her "rival" (1:6) oppressed her continually because of it. In the characteristic manner of a godly woman, she took her case to God in prayer. "The Lord remembered her" (1:19) and she gave birth to a son. She named him Samuel (1:20), which means "asked of the Lord." Prayer is effective. Isn't it about time that church people stopped talking about others and as James says, "Pray for one another"? The second case in which God used people is:

B. A Righteous Man, 5:16. James writes, "The effective prayer of a righteous man can accomplish much." This describes a man of faith (Rom. 1:17; Matt. 21:22). Commenting on this verse, Dr. Hoyt says:

> This makes the power of the prayer to depend not upon the righteous man, but upon God who works in the righteous man. God is the energizer (Phil. 2:13), and works in the righteous man "both to will and to do of his good pleasure." When He works in a man to pray, that prayer will accomplish much. It is powerful, for it pleases God.

The third situation of God's using people is the Old Testament illustration of:

C. Elijah, 5:17-18. The power of prayer is seen in the life of Elijah. He knew the secrets and resources of prayer. Listen to James: "Elijah was a man with a nature like ours, and he prayed earnestly that it might not rain; and it did not rain on the earth for three years and six months. And he prayed again, and the sky poured rain, and the earth produced its fruit."

I love this descriptive phrase of Elijah who was "a man with a nature like ours." Bible characters are not out of our league. They are just like us. When they sin, we can learn from their examples and sin not. When they are victorious, we realize that through Christ, we can achieve the same victories (Rom. 8:37). The Old Testament heavyweights were creatures of clay like you and I (I Cor. 10:11).

James says that Elijah was a "man." As a man, he possessed "a nature like ours." The idea is that Elijah went through the same experiences and sufferings of life that we do. Zodiates records:

> And this is spoken of the great prophet of God, Elijah. He prayed, and the soul of the widow's child returned to his dead body; but James reminds us that even he, Elijah, was a man of like sufferings and experiences with us. Affliction, sickness, and pain were his share. Though a man of God, he was not exempt from these experiences...The physician is subject to the same diseases he is able to heal. Elijah was the same nature as James and all of us. We are all made of one blood. Elijah was hungry (I Kings 17:11). He feared death and therefore fled from Jezebel (I Kings 19:3). He requested God to take his life when he became tired of living (I Kings 19:4).

Elijah is a super illustration of a man whose praying appropriates supernatural power. God responded in grace to do great things when this man prayed. James' words are: "...and he prayed earnestly that it might not rain; and it did not rain on the earth for three years and six months. And he prayed again, and the sky poured rain, and the earth produced its fruit." In simple terms, Elijah's praying *prevented* rain, and later he *provided* it (I Kings 17:1; 18:1). Hoyt comments further:

> So powerful were these prayers that nature moved at the word of this prophet of God, and an evil king and a whole nation bowed down to recognize that Jehovah is God. But the power of these prayers was not in Elijah but the God who wrought within Elijah. Remembering that Elijah was of like passions with us, and that it is God working in believers that produces powerful prayer, Christians should take heart and pray for the sick that they might be healed.

This is one of the most crucial areas of ministry for a believer to another believer—prayer!

VII. THE PURPOSES FOR GOD BRINGING SICKNESS TO PEOPLE, 5:19-20

"My brethren" is important to the understanding of verses 19 and 20. The word "brethren" appears over two hundred times in the New Testament and is a designation for the relationship of those who have trusted in Christ. Therefore what James is saying, he is saying to Christians. This is what he says, "if any among you strays from the truth," reveals that this straying can be done by a believer.

"Strays" is the Greek *planethei* from *planao*, "to wander." Our English word "planet" comes from *planao*. A planet is a wandering body and planetary means erratic or wandering. A Christian may wander or stray away "from the truth." This is a reference to Christ (John 14:6) and all that He has taught, which is known as the faith (I John 1:6; John 8:32; Jude 3). Yes, believers can become erratic and stray away from Christ and His teachings and His church; but, this condition cannot be permanent, else the individual was only *professing* faith and not *possessing* Christ (I John 2:19). There are generally three evidences that "straying" is occurring: (1) When a man leaves the church that he is attending for a negative reason; (2) When he stays in the church and becomes a part of the "carnal corral," which is the negative, retarding element; (3) When he develops moral problems.

Brethren, you and I are not "bullet-proof." We do not have an invisible guard or shield around us. We are susceptible to satanic attack. Hoyt warns, "And no Christian is in more danger of erring than that one who has already erred in thinking that he cannot err."

Again, the members of the body of Christ come into play. Wessel says:

> If a fellow Christian sees that his brother has left the great doctrines of the Christian faith and the moral responsibilities that spring from these, and is able to bring him back into fellowship with Christ and His Church, the consequences will be twofold: (1) he shall save a soul (the sinner's) from death, and (2) shall hide a multitude of sins.

The Scriptures are clear that a Christian can never forfeit his salvation. No one, at any time, in any way, has ever lost his salvation. A shocking truth is discoverable in II Timothy 2:13. Therein it states that if a Christian could lose his faith and deny Christ, God would remain faithful to him. Once God has predetermined a love relationship with an individual, God will forever remain true (Phil. 1:6). Salvation is of God and not of man (John 1:12-13). Election determines who the sheep are and insures their security. John 10:28-29 is filled with emphatics; for example, "...they shall never perish...." John chapter 10 is beautiful. In John 10:28 Christ's hands are mentioned. In John 10:29 the Father's hands are mentioned. Those are better hands than even All-State! Romans 8:33-39 is the classic passage on the subject of eternal security. So, beloved don't sweat your salvation. You're in good hands!—His hands!

Therefore, what James is discussing in 5:19-20 is church discipline.

Without being too coarse—when a believer gets out of line, God slaps him down on occasion. It is true that if a believer persists in sin, God may bring sickness and even death (I Cor. 11:30; I Cor. 5:1-5; I John 5:16). "He who turns" in verse 20 refers to a concerned brother who is able to cause a wandering brother to turn from his erratic behavior. Dr. Hoyt views it as follows:

> ...a complete about-face. And the only possible place where this may begin is with doctrinal error. The sinning saint must see God anew in all His holiness, he must see the exceeding sinfulness of his sin, he must see the dire consequences of proceeding any longer therein. A complete about-face from doctrinal error will also bring a complete about-face in the saint's way of life.

By doing this, the concerned Christian will perform an important feat for his wandering brother. Actually, he will "save his soul from death." One thing in common with false religious systems is that all of the adherents are attempting to earn their way to heaven. Hopefully good deeds on this earth will score "heaven points" and at death, these heaven points are weighed on the scales against the bad deeds. If the good outweighs the bad, then the one in question is admitted to heaven. Even certain Jews taught that the good deeds would offset the bad ones. (Again, James is using Hebraisms of which his Jewish audience would be well acquainted). That is the point of James' statement. The reclaiming brother is able to deliver, from divine discipline, the wandering one. In no way is this concerned Christian saved by means of this restorative deed (Eph. 2:8-9).

The phrase "Cover a multitude of sins" is also most intriguing. Again the dangerous doctrines of false religious systems are seen. For example, the Roman Catholic Church says that the concerned Christian, who reclaims the wandering brother, will save himself by saving others (Mayor and Ropes). Hoyt concludes:

> The ultimate effect of converting the sinner is that he will be saved from physical and eternal death. Personal sins, which may be the cause of physical illness, if not dealt with and done away, may bring one to the brink of the grave. In the anointing service these are dealt with. But even though God may not visit physical death upon a professed sinning saint, if he continues in sin, doctrinal and practical, he denies his profession and will ultimately not only suffer physical death but also eternal life.

> Let the saints praise God that through the avenue of physical sickness an opportunity has been provided in which the saint may be healed. But more important than that, it provides a place where inventory of one's spiritual state may be diagnosed and healed.

VIII. A POSTSCRIPT ON HEALING

Needless to say, there are healers abundant who profess healings abundant. What about these? May I suggest four sources of phenomenon: (1) God; (2) Satan; (3) Artificial stimuli; and 4) The flesh itself which may generate certain phenomena and emotional impulses. Whatever experience comes to the family of man, the source must be known in order to evaluate the validity of it. If the claimant espouses that the healing is of God, then the healing must be scrutinized under the careful exegesis of the miscroscope of Biblical scholarship. Anything which purports to be divine, must be able to stand up under the criteria of the Word of God. That just makes sense.

Healing is a captivating subject for all of us today. From the time one is born into this world, the process of decay is activated, and the individual zeroes in, as one man says, "On boxing day"; which is the day the individual meets the pine box. Death is simply the entrance of decay into the total expression of man. Then, one day, the immaterial part of man separates from the material part of man. Healing occupies, therefore, much of man's concern; because, while one is in the material body, he does all he can to maintain his dying, decaying body. Therefore, healing is an important entity in both the practice of medicine and religion.

To this point, it has been seen that God heals in His own particular way (James 5:13-20). Satan also heals (Matt. 7:21-23) through his phoney practitioners. Healing also may result from medicine and the use of drugs in the realm of artificial stimuli. The fourth area is the most crucial for our understanding of the faith-healing phenomena. This is the area of the flesh, the emotions and the psychological healing or psychotherapeutic or psychosomatic healings. This is simply the alleviating of the disorders of one's physical person which are directly caused by the mind. It is my humble opinion that this is the sphere where the faith-healer finds his willing subjects. This is the realm of the psychosomatic or psychological illness.

According to John MacArthur, some years ago, the Mayo Clinic stated that statistically 80 percent to 85 percent of their total case load were ill either in reality or artificially due directly to mental stress. Also according to MacArthur, not too long ago, there appeared an article in a leading medical journal entitled, "Is Stress the Cause of All Disease?" The author of the article says that at the beginning of the century, bacteria were considered to be the center of attention. Today, mental stress has replaced bacteria.

How can these things be? It is a strange phenomenon that certain emotions can alter and even change the actual functions of the human body. They cause such things as strokes, poisons, toxic goiters, blindness, fatal clots in the heart, bleeding ulcers in the intestinal tract, gangrene, kidney diseases, heart diseases, and others. All of the above and more can be very often attributed to stress and emotional and mental problems.

Dr. O. Spurgeon English, a medical doctor, published a very interesting book, describing how mental stress and the emotional center of the brain can cause debilitating and even fatal illnesses throughout the body. He demonstrates this by means of a series of diagrams, the first one being the drawing of a mental center, sending out nerve fibers to every area of the body. Due to the intricate nerve connections, it is explainable that any turmoil in the emotional-mental centers would transmit impulses that can cause anything to happen at the other end. The emotional center can transmit widespread changes, which can produce many things. For example, there can be a change in the flow of blood to an organ, which may result in physical problems. There can be a change in the muscles because of emotional stress which results in certain problems. Therefore, the cause and effect principle is readily seen. Some people are physically ill because they have a mental problem. Those who are under tremendous emotional and mental stress (sometimes creating their own stress) are exactly those to whom psychiatrists and faith healers lend their attention. The entire business of faith healing is wrapped up in this kind of illness.

Perhaps you have noticed the personality-type of a faith healer. He is, for the most part, always authoritarian, dynamic, aggressive, commanding and with a convincing presence. This is exactly what a psychosomatically ill person needs to hear—"You're healed!"—spoken from an authoritative voice. Obviously, these "healers" are able to release people from symptoms where there is no disease. Hypnotism is also involved to a great degree.

The story was released to the news media from Atlanta. It concerned a young boy who had been paralyzed and whose legs were in braces. He went to a "healing meeting." This "healer" went through the dramatics, put his hands on the boy's head, and said (only God knows what) and pronounced, "He's healed!" The emotion of the hour was so overwhelming that his parents removed the braces from the boy's legs and he "walked" down the platform, down the aisle and was seated. Within the span of two weeks, gangrene had set into his legs. It was *only* due to careful medical attention that the boy didn't lose both legs at the hip.

Just over a year ago, here in California, a faith healer "healed" a boy of diabetes. His parents threw away the child's insulin at the promptings of this fake. The boy died. His parents were arraigned on murder charges. I believe that the arraignment should have been made against the "healer." But, the "healer" said: "Have faith, your son will rise from the dead in seven days." The parents are still awaiting his resurrection.

Allow me to summarize by citing William A. Nolen, M.D., who is a noted doctor, skeptical, but willing to believe in the faith healers. He examined the phenomenon of faith healing, as practiced by the country's best known exponent, Kathryn Kuhlman (now deceased). He personally examined many of Miss Kuhlman's "healings" with her permission. His article "In Search of a Miracle" appeared in *McCall's*, September 1974. In the concluding words of Dr. Nolen:

> Kathryn Kuhlman's lack of medical sophistication is a critical point. I don't believe she is a liar or a charlatan or that she is, consciously, dishonest. I think she believes the Holy Spirit works through her to perform miraculous cures. I think she sincerely believes that the thousands of sick people who come to her services and claim cures are, through her ministrations, being cured of organic diseases. I also think—and my investigations confirm this— that she is wrong.
>
> The problem is—and I'm sorry this has to be so blunt—one of ignorance. Miss Kuhlman doesn't know the difference between psychogenic and organic diseases. Though she uses hypnotic techniques, she doesn't *know* anything about hypnotism and the power of suggestion. She doesn't know anything about the autonomic nervous system. Or, if she does know something about these things, she has certainly learned to hide her knowledge.
>
> There is one other possibility: It may be that Miss Kuhlman doesn't *want* to learn that her work is not as miraculous as it seems. For this reason she has trained herself to deny, emotionally and intellectually, anything that might threaten the validity of her ministry.
>
> I'm inclined to rest my case on the axiom, often used by the defense lawyer in malpractice cases when a sponge has been found in a patient's abdomen after an operation: *Res ipsa loquitur* ("The thing speaks for itself").

As one, among many, I have had enough of this "healing" myth. Let's get back to the Bible on the subject—James 5:12-20 is still in the Word of God. God heals *His* way and in *His* time. My wish for you is in the words of the beloved disciple, when he said, "Beloved, I pray that in all respects you may prosper and be in good health, just as your soul prospers" (III John 2).